CREATIVE MENTORSHIP AND CAREER-BUILDING STRATEGIES

Creative Mentorship and Career-Building Strategies

HOW TO BUILD YOUR VIRTUAL PERSONAL BOARD OF DIRECTORS

Mary Pender Greene, LCSW-R, CGP

OXFORD
UNIVERSITY PRESS

OXFORD

UNIVERSITY PRESS

Oxford University Press is a department of the University of Oxford.
It furthers the University's objective of excellence in research, scholarship,
and education by publishing worldwide.

Oxford   New York
Auckland   Cape Town   Dar es Salaam   Hong Kong   Karachi
Kuala Lumpur   Madrid   Melbourne   Mexico City   Nairobi
New Delhi   Shanghai   Taipei   Toronto

With offices in
Argentina   Austria   Brazil   Chile   Czech Republic   France   Greece
Guatemala   Hungary   Italy   Japan   Poland   Portugal   Singapore
South Korea   Switzerland   Thailand   Turkey   Ukraine   Vietnam

Oxford is a registered trademark of Oxford University Press
in the UK and certain other countries.

Published in the United States of America by
Oxford University Press
198 Madison Avenue, New York, NY 10016

Library of Congress Cataloging-in-Publication Data
Greene, Mary Pender.
Creative mentorship and career building strategies : how to build your
virtual personal board of directors / Mary Pender Greene, LCSW-R, CGP.
     pages cm
ISBN 978–0–19–937344–4
1. Mentoring in business.   2. Career development.   I. Title.
HF5385.G74 2014
650.1'3—dc23
2014022084

9 8 7 6 5 4 3
Printed in the United States of America
on acid-free paper

This book is dedicated to my Virtual Personal Board of Directors. A heartfelt thank you for the vital roles that you have played, and continue to play, in my life and career.

CONTENTS

9. Building a *Net* That *Works*   175

10. Serving on a Personal Board   188

FOREWORD

Mary Pender Greene has been a mentor, colleague, and friend for 20 years. She was an executive leader in one of the largest human services agencies in New York City for many years, where I worked and knew her as an experienced clinician, thoughtful manager, and respected mentor to many of my peers. In the last decade of her tenure at the agency, she led key aspects of a complex effort to implement a comprehensive strategic plan which included restructuring core aspects of the agency. This work required extensive networking and communication, delicate negotiations, respectful confrontations, and very high levels of trust with all the people involved. Mary and I collaborated closely in this work as it affected my division, and the years of partnership brought us closer and helped me to appreciate more fully the power of mentoring, both in developing my own career and in organization development.

A fundamental shift within the organization was to make the hierarchical structure transparent so others within the organization had a clear understanding, or at least access to the knowledge, of how decisions are made. Another important factor was taking advantage of teachable moments and other learning opportunities to help develop a diverse group of leaders from within the agency. Central to all of this was the need to develop meaningful and trusting relationships with a broad range of people connected to and invested in the organization. As a middle manager, running a program while working on the larger agency plan, I often thought of my work as negotiating tensions between "managing up" and "managing down" and was frequently frustrated with lack of movement in either arena. I wanted to support the type of change that would benefit my program and my division, *and* I wanted individual professional growth for my own benefit. Sometimes not seeing the forest for the trees, I struggled to recognize meaningful progress either for myself or for the organization. Mary's sage wisdom helped me see and optimize my impact through mentoring.

I learned to understand my work as a process of mentoring within a network of individuals committed to professional development—both my own and theirs. This proved to create a transformative perspective. Connecting with others through the lens of the mentor-protégé relationship, where roles are often complex and reciprocal, created numerous opportunities for learning and educating. One simple example of this occurs between Mary and me. I think of Mary as my mentor for a broad range of professional issues, and the internal question "How would Mary handle this?" is often present in my decision making or planning. She is also my clear go-to person for questions or concerns about intraorganization networking and negotiating delicate organization politics. She is, to use her words, my Chief Political Analyst. At the same time, Mary will come to me with questions or thoughts about diversity when she needs help responding to a subtle issue often related to micro-aggressions in a professional networking situation. I am one of her Diversity & Equity Officers. In this way, our mentoring is mutual; we each value the expertise and perspective of the other, growing and learning together and from each other.

Moving beyond the mentor-protégé dyad, I carry with me a group of mentors, my Virtual Personal Board of Directors, again in Mary's terms. This group has developed into a vibrant, constantly evolving relational matrix of brilliant, wonderful people with whom I am professionally connected. I can call on them anytime, reaching out by phone, text, or e-mail; setting up meetings; or making sure we connect when we are both at a conference or other professional event.

While many professionals may naturally hold a loose group of respected colleagues in their minds and reach out periodically, Mary's innovation is to create this group intentionally, as if we are creating a board of directors to help us run the business of our careers. Thinking about ourselves as entrepreneurs, regardless of our work role or setting, puts us in charge of the success of our "business"—the business of developing as a successful professional. Whom do you need as your Chief Financial Officer, advising on how to negotiate for a raise or helping you figure out if a new job with more pay but fewer benefits is the best long-term move? Whom do you know who would be your best Chief Technical Officer, helping you to make optimal use of a website, Facebook, or Twitter or figuring out which to emphasize in your marketing? Who should be your Education Officers, the people who will assist you in developing a continuing education plan or in figuring out how to keep your career momentum going as you return to school for an advanced degree or certificate?

For young professionals, those new to their careers at any age, this book offers insightful rules of engagement. You will learn how to get started making important connections that will carry you through to the success you envision for yourself. Your career started the minute you had that first dream, the goal, and the aspiration that got you through college, perhaps into graduate school, and set you on the path. Now you need to build the relationships that will continue your learning and development. Using the methods presented in this book, you will learn to build relationships outside of your organization to get anchored in the professional community. You are entering a profession, not just starting a job, and your long-term success will be built on the reputation that surrounds you, not just your skill at performing a function. Other people need to know about you, and other people will help you get where you want to be.

For mature professionals, those in middle or late career development who are looking for a way to create momentum to move into new roles or dig deeper to bring renewed vigor to their current roles, this book will help you build your power team. Building a team for professional development can be particularly challenging at the mid-career stage, when you may already be noted for achieving a level of expertise and have become the person others turn to for mentoring and support. Leveraging all of your professional relationships, with protégés, newer colleagues, advanced professionals, and peers, to learn the best of what they have to offer while imparting your professional wisdom forms a healthy foundation as you leap into the next phase of success. None of us is successful alone; people rely on others to develop and move forward professionally. Successful people are often good networkers who build relationships to move ahead. Therefore, the people you become connected to are also likely to be people who will value being connected to you. This book will show you how to nurture those relationships.

A good mentor gets excited about who they see you becoming without losing sight of who you are and helps you move forward and dig deeper to be your best. A creative mentor will help you look at the skills you already have and apply them to multiple aspects of your evolving career. In my case, Mary taught me that much of what I learned as a social worker, the quiet, reflective ability to build complex understandings of people and their environments which helped to explain conundrums and illuminate points for intervention, could be transformed into powerful skills for leadership in an organization. She also helped me recognize and frame my work as leader within a network of other leaders and potential leaders, so that networking and building toward collective success became a fluid part of how I do my job—any job.

Mentor relationships evolve over many years, and as interests and goals shift, the network of mentors is necessarily more complex. With this book, you will find methods for expanding your resources and a framework for lifelong success. Your career may be the biggest thing you ever build—so build something fabulous, make the foundation strong, and use your Virtual Personal Board of Directors as the structural frame to help you stand tall.

Lisa V. Blitz, PhD, LCSW-R
Assistant Professor,
Department of Social Work,
College of Community and Public Affairs,
Binghamton University
Associate Director,
Center for Family, School, and Community Partnerships,
Institute for Intergenerational Studies

INTRODUCTION

In today's economy, the stakes are high and we are all looking for an edge over the competition; with hectic schedules, we face major challenges when looking for a mentor. *Creative Mentorship and Career-Building Strategies* is a change in how we approach mentorship. No matter where you are on your journey—an ambitious student not yet in the work force, a new graduate seeking your first job, a seasoned professional looking to break out of mid-level management, or an experienced executive regrouping after being downsized—*Creative Mentorship and Career-Building Strategies* is a complete guide to tools that will help you make your goals a reality.

Written by Mary Pender Greene, a successful psychotherapist, career coach, and colleague, *Creative Mentorship and Career-Building Strategies* gives people from all walks of life a wealth of today's most effective mentoring, networking, and career development methods.

This guide is full of essential tips that have been put in a brief, informative, and interactive format, featuring the Virtual Personal Board of Directors (VPBOD) model, networking strategiesm and good old-fashioned advice for mentees and mentors. Some of the book's unique features include the following:

- Self-exploration worksheets
- The professional vision quest exercise
- Case studies in mentoring with a VPBOD
- Networking methods for the 21st century
- A complimentary online VPBOD Contact App for organizing and managing your professional network

With the Creative Mentorship method, you are free to tailor your experience to your needs. By looking through the table of contents, you can pick and choose sections that are especially useful to you. When used along with the exercises and the VPBOD Contact App, the tactics, case studies, and networking methods combine into a personal toolbox that I am confident will transform your approach to career development.

Terrie M. Williams
Author, *The Personal Touch:
What You Really Need to Succeed in
Today's Fast-Paced Business World*

ACKNOWLEDGMENTS

I thank my parents, Leon and Bertha Pender, sharecroppers and exceptional parents who taught me the power of the collective, relationships, love, and a positive attitude.

My siblings supported and nurtured me and pushed me forward as the family's hope. I was the 10th of 11 children, and my siblings were the basis of my first Virtual Personal Board of Directors long before I knew the words or the concept. I am blessed and eternally grateful that they all still live within a five-mile radius and continue to play that role today.

Ernest Greene—my husband, my best friend, my anchor—is a true visionary whose faith and vision gives me inspiration.

I thank Tiana Greene—my daughter and number one cheerleader—for her support, tenacity, forward thinking, and belief that her mom can do anything.

My son, Ernest Greene III, "Trey," who shows me the value of thinking outside the box daily and developed the app for this book.

Sharon Cohen of Ron Wood Public Relations, for her priceless knowledge, insight, and endless support. Her input and guidance have made this book a reality.

The wisdom and creativity of Margaret Santangelo, my associate editor, are immeasurable. I thank her for her contributions to this book.

I also thank Lynn Mercredi for her research, support, and endless patience during this process.

I am grateful to Oxford University Press for giving me this opportunity, with special thanks to Dana Bliss for putting out fires along the book's journey to press.

Thank you to my agent and advocate, Stacey Glick of Dystel & Goderich Literary Management, for taking a chance on this book and me.

Thank you to Alan B. Bernstein, who believed that a book was in my future years ago. He guided and supported me throughout my l-o-n-g journey.

I offer my gratitude to Ronald Chisom, David Billings, and the People's Institute for Survival and Beyond for teaching me the true meaning of networking. With special thanks to the PI collective, who are networkers building a net that works.

I acknowledge the Anti Racist Alliance, with special thanks to Sandra Bernabei for her tireless commitment to organizing via networking. Her skills and fortitude serve as a model for me.

The MPG Consulting Team offers evidence that my net works. I thank them for their expertise and dedication. To Lisa V. Blitz, Joan Adams, Sheilah D. Mabry, and the other members of my SWAT Team (you all know who you are), I am grateful for their being there for emergencies both big and small, and those six a.m. calls and e-mails. Terrie M. Williams, the ultimate connector, shared her network and her support.

I also thank NASW—NYC, NYS, and National—with special thanks to Robert Schachter and all social workers on the planet. Their networking saves lives, and I am very proud to be among their ranks. The former and current staff of JBFCS forms the nucleus of my professional family. Their collective wisdom is shared in the pages of this book. I give special thanks to the COR team. I owe thanks to all my former and current teachers, mentors, supervisors, bosses, and colleagues, many of whom fill the offices of my VPBOD. Their contributions are invaluable.

Finally, I thank all my former and current supervisees, students, mentees, and clients. Their wisdom, challenges, and triumphs provided the platform for my learning. Thank you for providing me with the opportunity to witness your growth and watch you thrive.

OVERVIEW

*C*reative Mentorship and Career-Building Strategies: How to Build your *Virtual Personal Board of Directors* is a hands-on workbook for professionals at all stages of their careers. *Creative Mentorship* introduces the **Virtual Personal Board of Directors (VPBOD)**, a comprehensive methodology for building and maintaining a professional network of mentors.

This system is practiced by Mary Pender Greene, LCSW-R, CGP, in her own career, through her work with patients, coaching clients, supervisees, and mentees. As a seasoned psychotherapist and licensed mental health professional, Pender Greene developed this system through her unique experiences in the fields of social work and psychotherapy. However, these methods are not limited to social work and mental health. The VPBOD mentorship system can easily be adapted for use by other professionals working in any number of fields. Imagine having intimate access to the experience and expertise of accomplished experts in wide-ranging areas vital to your career. The know-how of experts, from technical wizards and legal mavens to financial masterminds and political strategists, can all be available simply for the asking—*if* you maintain a well-rounded Virtual Personal Board. One distinct feature of Pender Greene's VPBOD system is that while other personal boards may be tied to your role at a specific organization, the VPBOD is not. Here you build your Virtual Personal Board over time and carry it with you throughout your career.

Although the system has been developed independently by Pender Greene during the past 20 years of her career, academics have simultaneously recognized the importance of "developmental networks" in the mentoring paradigm. In 1985, Kathy Kram of Boston University proposed that individuals look to more than a primary individual, or "mentor," for developmental assistance in their careers. Her research showed that individuals receive mentoring support from a set, or "constellation," of developmental relationships—from peers, subordinates, friends, families, and bosses. In short, mentoring is received from more than one single person (Kram, 1985, p. 181). In addition, Monica Higgins of Harvard University has conducted research in support of developmental networks, and the work of these two women provides a theoretical foundation for the VPBOD methodology.

Creative Mentorship and Career-Building Strategies: How to Build your Virtual Personal Board of Directors will accompany you on your journey to building, maintaining, and leveraging your VPBOD. Throughout this book, you will encounter interactive tools such as checklists, questionnaires, and fill-in-the-blank exercises. The aspiring professional should fill out the checklists and answer the questionnaires, as these exercises are provided to help you to build and maintain a VPBOD that works for you. This book is intended to be a roadmap for young, mid-level, and also seasoned professionals to build their own Personal Boards. This system is also useful for individuals who are considering a mid-career change, in order to help determine goals and aspirations. These may change over time (so you may want to use pencil), but don't skip over the interactive portions of this book. They are important tools designed to assist you on your road to professional self-discovery.

Throughout the book, you will be introduced to the stories of mentors and mentees who have used the tools and methods of the VPBOD in their own careers. These success stories will demonstrate exactly how, why, and when to implement the career-building strategies that make up this innovative professional networking and mentoring system.

HOW TO USE THIS BOOK

If you reviewed the table of contents, you probably noticed that the content in *Creative Mentorship* progresses in a linear fashion. An alternative title for *Creative Mentorship* could be "How to Create, Use, and Maintain a Virtual Personal Board of Directors." *Creative Mentorship* pursues the accomplishment of important pedagogical objectives such as presenting mentoring principles as defined in the current literature, demonstrating mentoring benefits by analyzing the relationships of well-known mentoring pairs, and illustrating the VPBOD methodology and core principles through anecdotal case studies and conceptual analysis.

However, taking you on the journey toward becoming the CEO of your own Personal Board is the primary purpose of this book—specifically, guiding you through the board-building process, advising you on the nuances of interacting with mentors, and demonstrating how best to leverage your Personal Board. *Creative Mentorship* accomplishes these didactic objectives by contextualizing the foundational pedagogy in an accessible "how-to" instructional format. Therefore, *Creative Mentorship* is structured for the primary purpose of outlining a step-by-step process for creating a VPBOD. *Creative Mentorship*'s other goals include establishing best practices for maintaining Personal Boards, reassessing the institution of mentorship in terms of contemporary work conditions, and encouraging the adoption of the VPBOD system by students, educators, and professionals.

The 10 chapters of *Creative Mentorship* fall into three main parts:

- Part I: Traditional Mentorship vs. the New Mentorship
- Part II: How to Build, Use, and Maintain Your VPBOD
- Part III: Progressing Professionally With Your Personal Board

Part I, chapters 1 and 2, consists of a review of traditional and contemporary mentoring models, with an emphasis on distinguishing between them and illuminating how new mentoring models accommodate recent changes in rapidly evolving and dramatically differing employment conditions facing the professional today.

Part II, Chapters 3 through 8, systematically describes the structure and features of the VPBOD system of mentorship, while also providing the theoretical foundations in support of the model. The content is presented in a progressive fashion, beginning with a big-picture point of view that introduces major concepts (Chapter 3), encourages you to reflect on your own professional goals (Chapter 4), and then narrows in on the nuts-and-bolts details of how to build, leverage, and maintain a Personal Board (Chapters 5 through 8). Throughout part II, you will find worksheets with the purpose of helping you create a Personal Board specifically tailored to your particular goals, career stage, and available resources.

Part III, Chapters 9 and 10, brings all the information from the preceding chapters together. Chapter 9 provides an in-depth analysis of networking, specifically in terms of the VPBOD system. Networking is fundamental to all aspects of the VPBOD mentoring methodology—from finding mentors to serve on your board to mining your board for connections—and is therefore the perfect topic by which to present a comprehensive synthesis of the concepts presented in part II. Chapter 10 suggests various means by which those who practice the VPBOD system can pay it forward by serving on Personal Boards themselves, as a means of advancing and spreading the VPBOD methodology into the future.

Creative Mentorship's step-by-step process for building, using, and maintaining a VPBOD is directly accessible by thoroughly examining and working with the various worksheets throughout the book. While there are worksheets in almost every chapter, those in part II, Chapter 5, are the most important in terms of setting a solid foundation for the later board-building process. Take the time to work on these worksheets and consider them seriously.

A complete index of names and topics provides lateral access to *Creative Mentorship*'s content, and a glossary defines important terms to which you may require quick access. Scattered throughout the chapters are inspirational quotes about mentoring that complement the broader concepts presented in the main text.

Creative Mentorship is an example of the new mentorship methodology, and its aim is to inspire members of both the new generation of professionals and previous ones to expand their horizons and adapt new ways of dealing with the rapidly evolving job market and professional milieu.

CREATIVE MENTORSHIP AND CAREER-BUILDING STRATEGIES

CHAPTER 1

MENTORSHIP YESTERDAY, TODAY, AND TOMORROW

You are the master of your destiny. You can influence, direct, and control your own environment. You can make your life what you want it to be.

Napoleon Hill

HOW YOU CAN BENEFIT FROM THE GUIDANCE OF A MENTOR

Author and motivational speaker Zig Ziglar once said, "A lot of people have gone further in life than they thought they could because *someone else* thought that they could." The simple fact is that capitalizing on the experience and advice of a mentor will improve your career potential. The main idea behind fostering mentorship within organizations, as stated back in 1978 in the *Harvard Business Review*, was that "Young people will have an older person in the organization to look after them in their early years to ensure that their careers are off to a good start. Out of these relationships, it is hoped that young people learn to take risks, accept a philosophical commitment to sharing, and learn to relate to people in an intuitive, empathetic way" (Ensher, 1978, p. 26). The professional landscape has changed dramatically since 1978, which is why I developed a unique mentoring strategy, the **Virtual Personal Board of Directors (VPBOD)**.

The purpose of maintaining a meaningful, ongoing relationship with a mentor is to have the wisdom of that certain someone who "thinks you can"—even when you may not. A **mentor** is a resourceful, well-connected supporter, an expert source of coveted information, and a wise advisor. A true mentor is, most important, someone who believes in you. If you want to succeed in your career and achieve your most ambitious professional goals, consider the many benefits of mentorship. According to Oprah Winfrey, a successful professional who credits her meteoric rise to the top to her close mentoring relationship with author Maya Angelou, "A mentor is someone who allows you to see the hope inside yourself. A mentor is someone who allows you to know that no matter how dark the night, in the morning joy will come. A mentor is someone who allows you to see the higher part of yourself when sometimes it becomes hidden to your own view" ("An Interview with Oprah Winfrey," 2002).

Consulting a mentor is a time-tested method for furthering both professional aspirations and personal goals. Through the institution of mentorship, knowledge is passed down, and valuable experiences are preserved for the benefit of subsequent generations. By working with a supportive mentor, young professionals gain confidence, knowledge, and proficiency in their chosen fields. By drawing on the knowledge of an experienced mentor, young professionals may avoid the mistakes and pitfalls of their predecessors.

Seasoned professionals who are more advanced in their careers can also benefit greatly by consulting mentors for advice and guidance. The more progress you have made in your career, the more crucial the decisions become. Determining your response to one job offer may completely change the direction of your entire career. In addition, even those who are happy right where they are will benefit from camaraderie with like-minded professionals. Mentorship plays a role at all stages of your career, no matter where you may be or where you want to go. Having a mentor is an asset for every professional in today's workplace.

MENTORSHIP: A HISTORICAL PERSPECTIVE

The institution of mentorship is the ages-old, time-tested bedrock of the continuity of almost every profession in our society. The benefits of experience cannot be understated when considering the journey into the unknown territory of choosing a career path. The classical definition of mentorship often cites the origin of the word *mentor*, which is derived from Homer's mythological character, Mentor, who looked after and educated Odysseus's son, Telemachus, while he was off fighting the Trojan Wars. This literary portrayal of mentorship was realized in real life in the seminal mentoring triad of Socrates, Plato, and Aristotle. (See "Profiles in Mentorship" section.)

Traditional mentorship is characterized by a one-on-one dyadic relationship, where the mentor is a wiser, more experienced individual who takes on the tutelage of a younger individual, usually in his or her own organization. According to Higgins and Kram (2001), "A 'traditional' mentoring relationship is one in which a senior person working in the protégé's organization assists with his or her personal and professional development." The classical mentorship approach would be monogamous; that is, the mentee would maintain the relationship with his or her mentor throughout his or her career, often following in the mentor's footsteps upon retirement and then continuing the cycle by taking on a **protégé** of his or her own. Traditional mentors provide three primary benefits to their protégés. First, they provide emotional support and a sounding board for their mentees. Second, they offer concrete career guidance in the form of advice and suggestions. Third, they present a role model for their protégé to refer to when making his or her own career decisions.

However, today's rapidly evolving professional landscape precludes the development of meaningful traditional mentoring partnerships. Employers expect—and often demand—that their staffers always be "on." The nine-to-five workday is a thing of the past; the workday continues after five and starts before nine. Professionals do not stay at one organization for their entire career. Frequent lateral job moves are now commonplace. Most people work both from home and from the office and are expected to be available via e-mail, chat, or Skype at all times. This is why traditional forms of mentorship are difficult to forge and maintain in today's workplace; there is not sufficient time or an accommodating atmosphere to develop and build a traditional mentoring relationship. Therefore, a new system of mentorship is needed for the 21st century, as supported by research studies. Theoretical work by Eby (1997) and Kram and Hall (1996) suggests that alternative forms of mentoring relationships (e.g., lateral relationships, mentoring circles) may be more or less helpful to individuals in adapting to organizational change.

All of these reasons provided the impetus for developing the methods and practices that make up the VPBOD mentoring system. It began as a solution to the difficulties I encountered in maintaining my own mentoring relationships, as both mentor and mentee. The significant success I observed in the implementation of the VPBOD system not only in my own career but also in those of my mentees inspired me to codify these methods and "pay it forward." In this book, I share my knowledge and experience with professionals both inside and outside of my professional practice.

THE BENEFITS OF MENTORSHIP

Despite mentorship being needed more and more in today's workplace, it is less available. The institution of mentorship is a continuous cycle that carries information, experiences, and resources down through the generations. Every mentor is likely a mentee; and every mentee will, it is hoped, be a future mentor. If you have a mentor, you can be sure that at one time or another, he or she was a mentee. In fact, your mentor is probably a mentee *right now*. The need for a mentor never ends; even after 30 years in a profession, we all need that cheerleader and trusted person we can ask for advice, the expert who seems to have all the answers. Even when mentors don't have the answers, they know someone who does.

Mentorship works best when there are clear benefits for mentors and protégés and also for their organizations and their professions as a whole. While mentors assist in developing the leadership capacity of mentees, they are also honing and developing their own skills. Mentoring helps to cultivate confidence, build and expand professional networks, and increase professional value. Mentors also contribute to and expand on the knowledge base of their profession as a whole for the benefit of future generations.

There are many benefits to both mentor and protégé. Some of the benefits to mentors are:

1. Gratification in fostering growth and helping others succeed.
2. Delegating tasks in order to free up your own time (if your mentee works with you).
3. Gaining new knowledge and insights.
4. Building a support network of like-minded individuals.
5. Expanding your professional perspective with board members who have a different perspective from your own.

6. Passing on knowledge and skills.
7. Helping a protégé to clarify his or her vision and achieve his or her goals.
8. Contributing to your overall profession.
9. Maintaining continuity and fostering growth in your field.

Some of the benefits a protégé can expect from mentorship are:

1. Developing a network of professionals in his or her field and beyond.
2. Having access to skills, knowledge, and experience beyond his or her years.
3. Gaining organizational know-how.
4. Increasing his or her professional wisdom and empathy.
5. Having someone in whom to confide.
6. Getting unbiased assessments of professional performance and progress, independent of a boss-employee relationship.
7. Gaining opportunities for promotion and advancement.
8. Getting honest feedback about skills and talents.
9. Developing authentic, open communication.
10. Having someone who can answer sensitive questions.
11. Gaining opportunities for increased visibility.

MENTEE TESTIMONIAL: HOW MENTORSHIP BUILDS CONFIDENCE

YOLANDA, 45, CLINICAL SOCIAL WORKER

"Ten years ago, I had advanced to middle management, and after 20 years in the field, I had just completed advanced training in organizational consultation. I was asked to be a speaker on the topic of leadership and women in the field. I had never done any public speaking and was nervous. I even considered turning down this valuable opportunity for increasing my visibility and credibility. Before dismissing this opportunity because of lack of experience and insecurity as a public speaker, I turned to one of my board members, a professor who had trained me in organizational consulting. She was able to help me with my speech and also bolstered my confidence. She made me feel sure that I could address a group of like-minded peers. In addition, she introduced me to other people in the field of organizational consultation and helped me expand my network. I am now a full-time consultant doing speaking engagements on a regular basis. Raising my profile as a public speaker introduced me to new people in the organizational consultation field. Because of my extensive connections, I have been able to go out on my own and generate enough business to consult full-time. I leveraged my VPBOD by reaching out to my former professor for support. It was the extra push I needed to reach my goal—and achieve an aspiration I didn't even realize was possible for me at that time."

WORKSHEET: ARE YOU READY TO BECOME A MENTOR?

Give yourself a score of 1 for yes, 0 for no. Add up the scores to determine your readiness to become a mentor.

1. Do you have a generous spirit?
2. Do you have good communication skills?
3. Are you interested in working closely with other people?
4. Are you interested in sharing your knowledge and experience with others?
5. Are you an honest person with a sense of integrity?
6. Do you enjoy witnessing others grow and evolve?
7. Do you enjoy teaching others?
8. Are you willing to share your network?
9. Are you open to using your influence to help others?
10. Are you able to have courageous conversations and provide opposing viewpoints?
11. Are you able to provide emotional and professional support?
12. Can you aid your protégé in preparing for courageous conversation?
13. Can you act as a role model for your mentee?
14. Can you teach your protégé to recognize and navigate office politics?
15. Can you enhance your protégé's sense of competence and self-esteem?
16. Can you help your protégé to maintain focus on his or her vision?
17. Can you educate your protégé in how to act like a leader?

RESULTS

If you scored a 12 or higher, you are ready to be a mentor.

WORKSHEET: ARE YOU READY TO BECOME A MENTEE?

Give yourself a score of 1 for yes, 0 for no. Add up the scores to determine your readiness to become a mentee.

1. Are you committed to becoming your best professional self?
2. Are you open to authentic communication?
3. Are you ready to take an honest assessment of your personality and goals?
4. Are you capable of follow-through?
5. Are you consistent and reliable?
6. Are you ready to make professional changes?
7. Do you currently have a clear vision for your professional future? If not, are you interested in creating one?
8. Are you open to the observations, criticisms, and suggestions of a mentor?
9. Are you aware of your gifts, talents, and positive characteristics?
10. Are you aware of your challenges and areas that could be developed?
11. Are you willing to explore the barriers that may be blocking your professional success?
12. Are you committed to developing an authentic relationship with your mentor?

RESULTS

If you scored an 8 or higher, you are ready to be a mentee.

THE RELATIONSHIP BETWEEN
MENTOR AND PROTÉGÉ

The most important factor in the relationship between mentor and mentee is that it is based on a foundation of mutual respect. The mentor-protégé relationship is also one of give and take. Both individuals should derive satisfaction and benefit from the relationship. The mentoring relationship will change and develop over time as the mentee becomes more self-reliant, competent, and confident.

In the past, one-to-one mentoring was the preferred and default definition of such a relationship. However, in today's career environment, there are new demands on mentor-protégé relationships that require a different approach. Rather than put all your eggs in one basket, a smarter approach to mentorship is to diversify the process strategically to get a large pool of skills, experiences, and knowledge. In this way, you will not rely too heavily on just one mentor. Kram (1985) originally proposed that mentoring relationships facilitate an individual's professional development by providing two types of "mentoring functions:" career functions and psychosocial functions. Career functions include sponsorship, exposure and visibility, coaching, protection, and providing challenging assignments; psychosocial functions include role-modeling, acceptance and confirmation, counseling, and friendship.

There are situations in which the traditional mentorship relationship does not provide sufficient guidance. It is important to maintain diversity in the types of people you depend on for the mentoring everyone needs throughout his or her professional life. It is important to foster diversity in both the types of individuals you consult with and the stages of their individual careers. The benefits of consulting many people rather than having just one mentor is that you will be able to garner advice from people who are different in addition to people who are very similar to you, so that you can get a lateral view of situations.

There is a void in mentorship in today's workplace. There are no longer consistent role models who you get to know over time. People need the benefits of mentoring not only for their own careers but also for the overall quality of work in the profession as a whole. A new system is needed for cultivating long-term professional relationships, and this need is exactly what the VPBOD strives to fill.

MENTORSHIP FOR TODAY
AND TOMORROW

The professional landscape has changed dramatically in the last three decades. Middle- and senior-level managers no longer enjoy the same stability in their positions that they once did. With changes in direction, limited funding for programs, restructuring, downsizing, and, of course, recession, mentors are just as likely to be downsized or laid off as their protégés. And if your claim to fame is being a certain someone's protégé, you may lose your job when he or she does. Connecting your future to a single rising manager has become an unwise and impractical career strategy. In the mental health field, and beyond, having just one mentor is often not enough. The true "superstars" don't have just one mentor; they have a Virtual Personal Board of Directors. A VPBOD is a "must-have" for navigating all the stages of a successful career in any profession. As a matter of fact, we need a VPBOD even more as we advance in our careers.

Pursuing professional growth by building and maintaining a VPBOD is a safer, and smarter, career strategy. A VPBOD enables you to draw on the strengths of many different people whom you admire and then synthesize the diverse input into your individual decisions. And as your career grows, so will your board, and you will be able to move the members around to different positions to suit your needs. There are different positions on your board, including a Professional Guru (see Chapter 3), who is the role model for your career. Maintaining a VPBOD means that you will have a diverse group of people to depend on throughout your career.

WHY A PERSONAL BOARD OF DIRECTORS FOR THE 21ST CENTURY?

There are four main reasons that using a **developmental network**, or VPBOD, is so important in the 21st-century workplace. Monica Higgins and Kathy Kram, in their seminal *Academy of Management Review* article "Reconceptualizing Mentoring at Work: A Developmental Network Perspective," identify them (Higgins & Kram, 2001):

1. The employment contract between individuals and their employers has changed (Rousseau, 1995). Job security has become a phenomenon of the past (Robinson, 1996, p. 574).
2. The changing nature of technology has also affected the form and function of individuals' careers and career development.
3. The changing nature of organizational structures affects the sources from which individuals receive developmental assistance.
4. Organizational membership has become increasingly diverse, particularly in terms of race, nationality, and gender, which affect both the needs and the resources available for development (Blake, 1999; Kram & Hall, 1996; Ragins, 1997a).

All of the above factors have contributed to the new professional landscape that has made traditional, one-on-one mentoring nearly obsolete. Proactive professionals, however, may overcome these difficulties by adjusting their career strategies and, most important, by building, maintaining, and leveraging a VPBOD.

THE BENEFITS OF NEW MENTORING MODELS

In this changing professional context, cultivating a developmental network, such as a VPBOD, is one of the most efficient ways to respond proactively to the challenges of today's professional landscape. The following are a few of the most important benefits of maintaining a Personal Board.

PROVIDING ACCESS TO DIVERSE PROFESSIONAL WISDOM

There isn't just one person with all the wisdom you may require. Most organizations will have two or three directives as determined by the corporate leadership that may or may not be your particular interest over the long haul. A VPBOD enables you to foster diverse interests beyond the limited scope of the top-down focus of your current organization. As your interests grow and change, you can maintain a diversity of professional skills even if you are working at an organization that is focused on other issues. A VPBOD will enable you to evolve as a professional and expand your initial specialties and interests.

MAXIMIZING TIME

In today's fast-paced world, very few professionals has enough time for a traditional mentorship relationship. There may not be time for weekly or monthly meetings. With a VPBOD, you require less time from each person by maximizing efficiencies. Since it is hard to make personal time, most people are hesitant to add something else to their plate by taking on a formal mentoring role. Being on a VPBOD could require as little as six hours a year or less. Mentees must be conscious of not requesting too much time. Because you have a range of different people to consult, you can cull the specific information you need from the right person when you need it. One key benefit of a VPBOD is that you have many different people available for consultation at all times. You need not worry about relying too heavily on one mentor and can therefore maximize the efficiency of your mentoring relationships.

ENCOURAGING PROFESSIONAL CONSISTENCY

In the past, people would grow professionally because they would be exposed to colleagues at work, such as bosses, supervisors, or coworkers, who helped to expand their knowledge base over time. If you had been in the field for a number of years with the same supervisors and a consistent professional leadership, you automatically benefited. When you work with the same people, your skills improve over time. In an environment where people change jobs frequently, every time the supervisor or the leadership changes, you are back to square one. In today's working world, you have to maintain professional consistency on your own, and a VPBOD is one way to accomplish this. When you make a connection at your organization, rather than let it expire when you go your separate ways, add this person to your VPBOD so you can continue to work with him or her proactively and maintain a professional connection. There are many ways to accomplish this, such as working together on professional articles or participating in conferences and workshops together. Seasoned professionals appreciate a mentee's assistance with projects and show that appreciation by taking special interest in the mentee's career. For example, a mentee might offer a mentor help with his or her presentation and ultimately co-present at an international conference—with potential benefits such as a paid trip and credit in the presented materials. Mentees should always be looking for ways to help mentors, such as with research, social media, or administrative tasks. Even small contributions can make a big difference.

MAINTAINING RELATIONSHIPS

Since people are always moving around, it is difficult to build long-lasting relationships at one organization. Every time you move to a new job, you don't know the strengths of the people you work with, and they won't know your strengths. Each time that happens, your career development is affected. By adding important colleagues to your VPBOD, you are able to maintain that source of knowledge past your time together at a particular organization. You will also be able to obtain references after career shifts are made by you or others.

CASE STUDY: EXPANDING YOUR MENTORING NETWORK WITH A PERSONAL BOARD

> Nothing more, nothing less, therapy is the art of teaching someone to overhear himself.
>
> Stephen Metcalf

In this case, a mentor guides Alexandra, 37, a mid-career hospital administrator, to build a Personal Board when she unexpectedly loses her job—and her confidence.

Alexandra, 37, an experienced director of training at a hospital, was fired after ten years at the same organization. As the director of training, Alexandra prepared course materials and curriculum, hired lecturers and trainers, and maintained course registration and scheduling. In addition, she was responsible for ensuring that hospital staff stayed up-to-date with training courses required for compliance with regulations. However, she was a "people pleaser" who desperately wanted to be liked by everyone, and staff management was not one of her strong suits. Instead of being extra-vigilant with employees who fell behind in mandatory coursework, Alexandra failed to hold them personally accountable. She also concealed their training deficiencies from upper management. As a result of her clouding of facts and covering for employees, Alexandra was fired. Like many others at her level, she had grown comfortable and idle in her position and uninspired by and neglectful of her career. She was completely blindsided by the firing. Had she been paying closer attention to her career, she would have seen it coming.

When Alexandra lost her job, she felt hopeless, rejected, and lost. Because she was fired for cause, she was unable to ask her bosses for professional recommendations. She worried about next steps. She not only needed solid references, but she also needed to clean up her act so she could move on in a positive direction.

Alexandra came to me for advice about what she could do. As her mentor, I first wanted to know:

1. What skills could Alexandra transfer to a new position?
2. What were Alexandra's professional goals right now?

My strategy was to focus her on pursuing the following:

1. Making an honest assessment of both her gifts and her challenges.
2. Sharpening her future professional vision through self-reflection.
3. Exploring her goals and determining where her passions lay.

It became evident to me that the director of training position was not one of her initial career goals. The hospital had asked her to do this job because there was an opening, but it was not actually what she *wanted* to do. So, therefore, she did have other options. She was really interested in being a researcher, but the hospital needed to fill the role of director of training and the position came with a higher salary, so she took it, despite the fact that it was *not* the career path she would have chosen for herself. The other questions I asked Alexandra to consider were: What did she do before her director of training job? What were her professional aspirations at the start of her career? Where would she like to see herself ten years from now?

Because she was fired, Alexandra's self-esteem was devastated, and she completely lacked confidence in her abilities. I helped her to examine her need to be liked. I shared with her my observation that she, like many other women, had a strong desire to be liked. Some will do anything to be liked while striving for respect. We talked about shifting her focus toward optimal performance, which earns respect. The priority should be on being respected before being liked. People not only respect you but like you more if you're both honest and proficient. She came to realize that a deeply etched need to be liked is a serious handicap to any leadership role.

The next step I took was to coax Alexandra into thinking about colleagues—outside her time at the hospital—and other people in her life who had believed in her and supported her: professors, friends from college, former employers, professional peers. I suggested that she reach out to these people and set up appointments to meet with them. This was the first step in guiding Alexandra on the journey of developing her own Personal Board.

Alexandra then met with a variety of people and realized that while she had filled the director of training role at the hospital, it was not her primary interest in the field and that because of her responsibilities as director of training, she had stopped pursuing jobs pertaining to clinical research, the direction she initially wanted to pursue after earning her degree. I recommended that she contact other people who were conducting research so she could get up to speed with the field. Through one of the peer colleagues on her developing Personal Board, Alexandra was informed of an open researcher position. She is currently part of a research team and is looking to develop her career in a clinical setting rather than in an administrative role.

Because Alexandra had no real passion for administration, it was naturally difficult for her to excel in that capacity. There were sacrifices to be made: at her new position, her salary was lower, she was not in a director role, and she had to pursue continuing education independently in order to get up to speed. However, she truly enjoyed what she was doing and knew she would regain her salary in an area where she was better suited. The board helped Alexandra to realize that "people pleasing" is the enemy of effective leadership and that she needed to focus on being respected, not liked. Suggesting that mentees get help with issues that stall or hold back their careers is part of a mentor's role. In this case, I referred Alexandra to a therapist and suggested that she consult her gut first and her board members second before making future career decisions. I also offered her "feedforward"—a type of constructive criticism—about her need to encourage and seek respect from her colleagues and employees rather than be liked by them. But most significantly, I gave Alexandra the emotional support she needed.

What a mentor does is help the mentee stay focused on aspirations and hopes for the future in order to guide him or her on the proper path. However, the Chairperson of a Virtual Personal Board goes the extra distance by helping the mentee create his or her own Personal Board in order to stay on the path toward fulfilling his or her dreams.

FAMOUS MENTORING PAIRS: HISTORICAL FIGURES

Mentor	Mentee
Archimedes, ancient Greek mathematician	Galileo, Italian astronomer
Aristotle, classical Greek philosopher	Alexander the Great, King of Macedonia
Julius Caesar, ancient Roman dictator	Mark Antony, Roman politician and general
John Dewey, American philosopher	Sidney Hook, American philosopher
Elijah, Israelite prophet	Elisha, Israelite prophet
Galileo, Italian astronomer	Ferdinand II, Grand Duke of Tuscany
Brunetto Latini, Italian philosopher	Dante Alighieri, Italian poet
Marie de Médicis, Queen of France	Cardinal Richelieu, French clergyman
Plato, classical Greek philosopher	Aristotle, classical Greek philosopher
Cardinal Richelieu, French clergyman	Jean Desmarets de Saint-Sorlin, French writer
Augustin Robespierre, French revolutionary	Napoleon Bonaparte, French military leader
Saul, King of the Hebrews	David, King of ancient Israel
Socrates, classical Greek philosopher	Plato, classical Greek philosopher

PROFILES IN MENTORSHIP:
SOCRATES, PLATO, AND ARISTOTLE

The mentoring trio of Socrates, Plato, and Aristotle is one of the most influential historical profiles in the institution of mentorship. Along with his mentor, Socrates, and his student, Aristotle, Plato was one of the seminal minds who laid the foundation for Western thought and its corresponding educational system. This early chain of mentorship served to pass down seminal concepts and philosophies from one generation to subsequent generations and thus established a completely new way of thinking. The mentoring relationships between, first, Socrates as mentor to Plato and, then, Plato as mentor to Aristotle informed the entirety of Western thought.

The concepts and teachings of Socrates were considered so radical in his time that he was eventually executed for corrupting the youth of Athens, and had he not fostered a close intellectual relationship with protégé Plato, his revolutionary ideas may have died with him. However, Plato carried on the work of his mentor, Socrates, and in effect rescued a philosophy intrinsic and foundational to our current pedagogical system, specifically the Socratic method, which informs the majority of educational methodologies being practiced to this day.

Subsequently, Plato took on a close protégé of his own, Aristotle, in an effort to continue propagating Socrates's important philosophies. Aristotle studied under Plato at his Academy for 20 years and was Plato's heir apparent despite the fact that he argued with his mentor about several philosophical issues. Aristotle went on to tutor and mentor Alexander the Great for seven years starting when Alexander was 13. Aristotle eventually established the Lyceum, a mental gymnasium, where students exercised their minds instead of their bodies. The Lyceum proved to be a model for the university system as we know it today. Socrates, Plato, and Aristotle had a profound influence not only on the institution of mentorship but also on higher education in our society.

KNOWLEDGE NUGGETS

- The Virtual Personal Board of Directors (VPBOD) is one of the most effective systems of mentorship for the 21st century.
- Mentoring helps to cultivate confidence, build and expand your own personal network, and increase your sense of professional value.
- There are situations in which the traditional mentorship relationship does not provide sufficient guidance.
- Having just one mentor is often not enough. The true "superstars" don't have just one mentor; they have a VPBOD.
- A VPBOD is a "must-have" for navigating all the stages of a successful career in any profession.
- There are three reasons building a VPBOD is the best method of maintaining mentoring relationships in the 21st century: (1) it affords access to a wide range of professional wisdom, (2) it enables busy professionals to maximize their time, and (3) it facilitates organizational consistency and continuity.

CHAPTER 2

THE BASICS OF THE NEW MENTORING MODEL

Mentoring is a brain to pick, an ear to listen, and a push in the right direction.

John Crosby

A MENTORING REVOLUTION

The new mentoring model, as typified by the Virtual Personal Board of Directors model, broadens and advances the definition of mentorship. The VPBOD methodology expands significantly on the traditional definition of mentoring relationships as dyadic (one-on-one), monogamous, and hierarchical. This new mentoring model, represented by the VPBOD, is rooted in the basic concepts of traditional mentorship but also identifies a variety of mentoring relationships. It also demonstrates a methodology for the creation and management of these relationships.

Most significantly, the VPBOD confirms that monogamous and dyadic mentor-protégé relationships are a thing of the past. The professional landscape of the 21st century demands a more complex and detail-oriented approach to mentorship. Today's professionals require more than one mentor to fulfill the developmental and psychosocial support required in today's insecure and highly competitive employment environment. The VPBOD is a construct that encourages individuals to build a circle, or "constellation" (Kram, 1988), of mentors around themselves on whom they can rely to fulfill differentiated and specialized needs. Each of these mentoring relationships is tailored specifically to the needs of an individual at any given point in time and managed through the VPBOD construct.

In addition to increasing the number of mentoring relationships an individual may maintain simultaneously, the VPBOD also does away with the concept that all mentoring relationships should be hierarchical or that a mentor must be more professionally advanced or of a higher title than his or her protégé. Lateral, or peer mentoring, relationships are just as important as those of a hierarchical nature. In addition, reverse mentoring, defined as a younger person acting as mentor to someone more professionally advanced, is included as an important modality in the VPBOD model.

Aside from evolving beyond these two central tenets of traditional mentoring, the mentoring revolution introduces a dynamism and vibrancy to the relationship between mentor and protégé as never seen before. Aside from not only having multiple mentors and not being limited to only superiors, the new mentoring model encourages self-driven and proactive individuals to pursue what Douglas T. Hall calls the "boundaryless career." This term, along with the "protean career," denotes career aspirations with no limitations or restrictions that would traditionally be imposed by the rigorous hierarchical structures of the past. The VPBOD is a methodology you can employ in pursuit of the boundaryless career because of its versatility and accommodation of many different, distinct, and directed mentoring relationships.

The leading scholarship regarding the system of maintaining multiple mentors is represented by the work of Mary Higgins, Kathy Kram, and Lillian T. Eby. It has been proven, through research studies, statistical analyses, and anecdotal case histories, that implementing mentoring methodologies along the lines of the VPBOD model represents a significant asset for a 21st-century professional and will enable him or her to advance more quickly, adjust more easily, and navigate more confidently the rocky terrain of the changing employment environment:

> Mentoring was differentiated based on the form of relationship (lateral and hierarchical) and the type of skill developed (job-related and career-related). In so doing, the construct of mentoring was expanded to include ways it can help individuals and organizations adapt to a changing workplace. By updating the construct of mentoring to reflect current career trends and providing an agenda for future research, avenues are suggested for taking mentoring research and practice into the next century.
>
> Eby, 1997, p. 42

In traditional mentoring relationships, mentors support mentees in three ways: offering career guidance, providing emotional or psychosocial support, and serving as effective role models (Ensher & Murphy, 2005, p. 29). The mentor-mentee relationship was limited to a wiser mentor advising a younger, less experienced protégé. In the new mentoring models, such as the VPBOD, mentors provide all of the above types of support to their protégés but in a less rigid context that permits mentees to maintain relationships with multiple mentors, who may or may not fit into the definition of a traditional mentor.

However, the traditional mentoring model should not be discarded or dismissed; in fact, many aspects of the one-on-one relationships between mentors and mentees in the VPBOD system rely on the principles developed and perfected in the dyadic traditional mentoring model. The main difference is that traditional mentorship constricts the possibilities for a protégé to access knowledge and advice, and the VPBOD encourages a professional to branch out and seek multiple mentors from various areas to support his or her professional goals. In addition, in traditional mentoring relationships, it is usually the mentor who approaches the protégé and "takes him or her under his wing," implying that mentees are not the initiators of mentoring relationships. In the VPBOD system, this is the complete opposite: mentees are often the initiators of the mentoring relationship, and much of the board-building process focuses on this precise objective. In this way, using the VPBOD system encourages mentees to take a proactive role in connecting with mentors and building those relationships. Just because you use a Personal Board to maintain your mentoring relationships, that doesn't mean you can't also seek out a more formal, traditional mentoring relationship, especially within your organization. Since the Personal Board is a mental construct and your board members are not formally aware of their positions, establishing a traditional mentoring relationship with a superior within your organization could be quite beneficial to your career. A boss-mentor may be able to share privileged information or teach you new skills that will improve your job performance or even make you eligible for promotions and choice assignments. Such relationships may also enhance the chances of a being sponsored, which is the ultimate goal of many mentor-mentee relationships.

TYPES OF MENTORS

THE BOSS-MENTOR

The boss-protégé relationship is a remnant of the traditional dyadic mentoring modality. Usually, if a supervisor especially likes and trusts a subordinate, he or she will establish a boss-mentorship. A **boss-mentor** is very much like a sponsor, except that boss-mentoring relationships usually end when either the boss or the protégé leaves the organization. Usually, the boss is grooming the protégé to succeed him or her, thereby ensuring continuity in the organization. While having your boss as your mentor can bring many benefits, such as emotional, professional, and practical support in your position, keep in mind that your relationship depends on your common employment at the same organization. Moreover, the protégé's professional success depends on the performance of the boss-mentor (Ensher & Murphy, 2005, p. 47), so as your boss-mentor's star rises or falls, yours will do so along with it. However, one of the benefits of a VPBOD is that you maintain professional independence with respect to boss-mentors. In addition, appointing a boss-mentor to your Personal Board rather than relying on him or her as your primary mentor encourages you to continue the relationship after one of you departs the organization.

THE eMentor

When you use technology to expand your mentoring possibilities, connecting with potential mentors or protégés via social networks, online communities, or other Internet-based communication means, this is **eMentoring**. While eMentoring has the advantages of removing the constraints of time and geography, there are also disadvantages, such as the potential for miscommunication and misrepresentation. Also, eMentoring can remove the markers of status and demographics, making mentors and protégés more likely to respond to the content of their messages, rather than being influenced by superficial characteristics. An eMentorship approach can help to expand and enhance your relationships with your VPBOD. Using technology can greatly increase your access to your board, increasing your access to resources, information, and **eIntroductions**.

THE GROUP MENTOR

A **group mentor** is a senior-level executive who mentors a group of junior-level employees. Group mentoring can take place within the context of an organization or a specific field. Group mentoring is especially useful for a mentor who is extremely busy and in high demand by many potential protégés; in the setting of a group, scheduled to meet on a regular basis, a highly sought-after mentor can provide guidance to a group of people simultaneously, thus maximizing his or her time and reach. Larry Carter, CEO of Cisco, uses the group-mentoring approach, calling it "Lunch with Larry," during which he meets with 10 to 12 junior employees. He explains: "There's no agenda, and it's just me and the people. They are usually from different parts of the organization. There is no better way than to sit down, look them right in the eye, and tell them the good, the bad, and the ugly. You develop a rapport, and you also make them feel comfortable" (Ensher & Murphy, 2005, p. 51). Group mentoring is not only a useful tool when a busy executive has too many potential protégés to mentor, but it is also useful for establishing a sense of camaraderie within an organization and fostering peer mentoring among the protégés.

Another approach to group mentoring is for a senior person to organize mentoring groups outside an organizational context, centering the group on common professional challenges. In the context of a Personal Board, either the mentee or the board member may recognize situations where gathering as a group would benefit both the mentor, by maximizing his or her time, and the mentees, by fostering peer connections and facilitating dialogue and support among professionals in similar positions and careers.

THE MENTOR-FOR-HIRE

You may consider adding a **mentor-for-hire**, or career coach, to your Personal Board if there is a specific area that you must urgently address in order to advance your career. Although maintaining a relationship with a career coach over the long term is always helpful, it can prove too costly for the entry-level junior employee. However, if you find you are having difficulty filling a specific slot on your Personal Board for some time and require the specialized guidance of a mentor in a specific area, such as building a website or acquiring a certification that will enable you to advance professionally, a mentor-for-hire may be a stopgap measure. A mentor-for-hire should be considered a short-term solution until you are able to identify a board member, most likely through networking with current members, to fulfill this need for the long term. Until then, a paid coach can complement your growing VPBOD and may be instrumental in helping you to further expand your board through brainstorming and making connections.

THE INSPIRATIONAL MENTOR

Inspirational mentors are role models for their protégés, providing examples on which they may model the development of their own careers. Inspirational mentors provides mentees with a sense of identity, purpose, and vision by virtue of their outstanding accomplishments in their fields and professions. A mentee may be inspired by an invisible mentor, such as someone whom the protégé may never be able to meet because he or she is famous or no longer living. On the other hand, inspirational mentors can also be real-life accessible individuals with whom the mentee can interact. Inspirational mentors are a key to the productive application of role-modeling by mentees in order to develop their own sense of direction and purpose in their own careers.

THE FAMILY-MEMBER MENTOR

An immediate- or extended-family member who is especially admired by relatives is often a good choice for a board member. You can be sure these people have an emotional stake in your success, and you have the added benefit of being familiar and comfortable with them, making your relationship very genuine. While anyone can benefit from a **family-member mentor**, women and people of color especially may rely on them when their professional network does not include many people similar to them in gender, race, or ethnicity. Trusted family members who have achieved career success can offer important advice on navigating issues that come up around sexism, institutional racism, or subtle aspects of organizational culture that unintentionally marginalize women and/or people of color. Similarly, gay and lesbian people may seek mentors from a "family of choice," a network of close friends who understand the stress of managing homophobia and heteronormativity (cultural bias as part of a worldview that promotes heterosexuality as the normal or preferred sexual orientation) in the workplace. Family-member mentors offer the added benefit of knowing more about your personal life and history than other members of your VPBOD and may offer guidance and advice in more personal ways.

THE BARRIER-BUSTING MENTOR

Mentoring relationships often develop between people of similar backgrounds and within similar organizations and affiliations. A relationship with a **barrier-busting mentor** forms across traditional organizational divides—for example, a Republican mentoring a Democratic candidate for office. Other examples include Hilda Solis, a Latina, mentoring Judy Chu, a Chinese American. These types of unlikely mentoring partnerships challenge accepted values and push the envelope.

THE PEER MENTOR

The **peer mentor** is someone who is close to your own age and career level to whom you can turn for psychosocial support in difficult situations. The person may or may not be in your field, although peer mentors who share your profession will be more helpful when it comes to specific issues pertaining to your job. Peer mentors are especially helpful in a group context, such as an institutional mentoring program in which a more experienced mentor counsels more than one individual at the same time, because you will all be sharing similar experiences and can either commiserate about problems or enjoy one another's success. Cross-professional peer board members are also useful in that they can give you a perspective on what other professions are like. It is important to have a mix of people, demographically speaking, on your board, and you should be sure to include peers. A peer support group is one form of peer mentorship that provides psychosocial support. For example, three female colleagues at the same company but who report to different bosses could meet once a month to discuss work and professional progress over lunch.

One of my executive-coaching clients set up a peer-mentoring group with four female colleagues who were executives in the nonprofit sector. They were all isolated and overworked. The group developed as a result of a dinner and morphed into a peer group that met monthly. They put it on their calendars as a recurring appointment. They brainstormed ideas and discussed strategies, opportunities, and office politics and gave one another inspiration and moral support. Some outcomes from the connection were as follows:

- One member found members for her nonprofit's board.
- Many found candidates for open positions, leading to hiring solutions.
- One member gained strategies to help her deal with the difficult chair of her agency's board.
- They began going to karaoke as a group, providing much-needed socialization, since none had an active social life.
- They each agreed to hold one another accountable for keeping their résumés updated and available for new opportunities.

One member sponsored the application of another by personally presenting it to the hiring manager for a senior VP position, a major step up that she had not been seeking but which catapulted her career to a new level.

THE SITUATIONAL MENTOR

A relationship with a **situational mentor** arises out of common circumstances, such as working on a project together, attending the same class, or belonging to the same professional organization. This is similar to situational friendships, such as those with neighbors that arise out of shared proximity rather than having things in common. By definition, these relationships usually dissolve when the shared situation ends, such as when you move away from your neighbor in the case of a situational friendship or when you leave a certain organization with a situational mentoring relationship. However, situational mentors can have a great impact on your career development.

Situational mentorships arise out of work situations that are short-lived and project-based (Ensher & Murphy, 2005, p. 62) and have natural predetermined endings. Often context-specific, situational mentorships may be limited to the time individuals are brought together (Ensher & Murphy, 2005, p. 62). What protégés learn from these "mentors of the moment" can be career-changing and dramatic, such as when you have the opportunity to work with a legendary figure in your industry. For example, film director Lesli Linka Glatter once worked with Steven Spielberg, which she described as a seminal experience for a young director, one that changed her career path dramatically. You must be proactive in appointing a mentor of the moment to your Personal Board immediately and pursue opportunities that will enable you to potentially become close to influential individuals. Mentors of the moment can provide you with invaluable information, especially when working closely together on a challenging project. Identifying and pursuing situational mentors for your Personal Board will enable you to advance your career and increase your knowledge.

MENTORING MODALITIES

Various mentoring modalities have arisen out of the new mentoring model. The following new ways of mentoring are available to you and your board members as part of the VPBOD methodology.

DYADIC (ONE-ON-ONE) MENTORING

The foundation on which all mentoring modalities are based is the traditional mentoring model, referred to as **dyadic mentoring** or one-on-one mentoring: "A 'traditional' mentoring relationship is one in which a senior person working in the protégé's organization assists with the protégé's personal and professional development" (Higgins & Kram, 2001, p. 265). Despite the development of various new mentoring methodologies, such as those that follow, the dyadic mentoring modality continues to be the central, foundational mode on which all mentor-mentee relationships are based. Despite the variations and innovations that have developed for the 21st-century employment environment, such as speed mentoring and one-minute mentoring, the core dynamic is based on a dyadic (or one-on-one) relationship between two people—protégé and sponsor, student and teacher, mentor and mentee—specifically entered into in order that the more experienced and knowledgeable of the two can pass knowledge, experience, and skills on to the other.

REVERSE MENTORING

Reverse mentoring is an initiative in which seasoned executives are paired with and mentored by younger employees on topics such as technology, social media, and current trends. In the tech industry or other businesses that rely heavily on technology, reverse mentoring is seen as a way to bring more mature employees up to speed in areas that are often second nature to 20-somethings, whose lives have been more deeply integrated with computers and the Web. This is the organizational definition of reverse mentoring;

however, in the VPBOD methodology, it is different, because it is on a more personal level. Reverse mentoring takes on an additional significance in terms of the way mentoring relationships work between more mature mentors and younger mentees.

Mentoring is a two-way street. Reverse mentoring is an institutional practice, but you can apply it to yourself. However, you should be constantly assessing how you can be helpful to your board member, not returning favors quid pro quo. Don't keep score of your favors. Generosity is the key to successful mentoring relationships.

Age and experience are not the issue. Focus on fostering a reciprocal relationship. No matter who the mentor is or how old he or she is, it is helpful to think about how you can help your mentor by contributing your time and effort. The expected payment for being a part of a professional posse/mentoring community is that you pay it forward and look for opportunities to give back, not just to your mentor but also to others who are referred by members in your network.

Specific ways to help your more mature mentors include volunteering to do certain low-commitment tasks such as helping with their research projects, attending their speeches, suggesting that they offer webinars, or auditing their websites. Volunteering to provide a service that helps you strengthen one of your own skills or builds your résumé is ideal. For example, Jiang volunteered to conduct a survey for a board member on the consultant fees that were being paid to psychologists by local mental health agencies. The survey results could be used for a paper Jiang was writing for a graduate research class. It was a win-win.

INVISIBLE MENTORING

The **invisible mentoring** modality enables you to access and implement the assistance of people you don't know or cannot access, such as celebrities or hotshots in your field, by appointing them to your Personal Board. The most important task in including invisible mentors on your board is to research everything you can about them, including their biographies, their mentors, and their philosophy. You can utilize an invisible mentor's most important qualities and achievements to inform your own personal and professional development and your own career choices. Over time, you may sometimes be able to develop an actual relationship with your invisible mentors. But in the meantime, you can still profit from utilizing them as not just role models but also as board members.

You can connect with invisible mentors by following and becoming a fan of their work. One way to do this is to follow them on social media and blogs and participate in the discussions. In this way, you may be able to distinguish yourself and be noticed.

You can also profit from the examples of individuals you look up to from the past through the principles of invisible mentorship. For example, Hillary Clinton considered Eleanor Roosevelt a major influence and role model for her career, and despite their separation in time, she was still able to use Roosevelt as a role model to guide her current career. Another way invisible mentoring can be quite useful is for modeling your professional development after that of a celebrity or high-profile colleague to whom you have no possibility of access. You can still benefit from looking at such people as role models and mentors, by studying their professional choices, absorbing everything you can about them, and following their careers closely.

WAYS TO WORK WITH INVISIBLE MENTORS

- Research biographies and autobiographies about your invisible mentors.
- Conduct research to identify the writing, speeches, and presentations given by and about your invisible mentors, including in periodicals, journals, books, and videos.
- Through your research, identify themes in their lives and work.
- Find out and make a list of who *their* mentors were, especially how they landed their "big breaks" and which mentors, if any, were instrumental.
- Identify and become familiar with their central philosophies.
- Discover in what ways are they similar and dissimilar to you.
- Learn how your invisible mentors move past challenges and generate ideas.
- Identify the 10 greatest ideas your invisible mentors used in their careers.
- Figure out how can you apply the principles they lived by to your work and life.

ONE-MINUTE MENTORING

With **one-minute mentoring**, you can get information quickly from people who may not be accessible in a long-term sense, such as after a speech they give when you have one moment to connect with them. Different ways of connecting along the lines of one-minute mentoring can range from the quick check-in to an annual two-hour lunch.

Quick-check mentoring allots enough time to receive insight but is short enough to fit into a busy schedule. It is used to address a specific goal. The purpose is to lift your spirits, keep you focused, or to get a pep talk. You can use it as a confidence booster for your first big keynote speech or interview. This modality requires that the mentor is already somewhat familiar with the situation.

Speed mentoring, which comes from Dana Perino's award-winning Minute Mentoring program, is a unique, round-robin-style forum in which accomplished female professionals share their experiences with their young professional counterparts during rapid-fire meetings. Similar to speed dating, small groups of mentees rotate among mentors, allowing for a large group to network while maintaining the intimacy of mentorship.

Three female attorney members of my coaching group arranged for a women-only speed-mentoring event at an international law conference. More than 85 female attorneys from all over the globe attended the mentoring event. It was a massive success, since most of the attendees worked in a male-dominated setting and had limited chances to expand their international connections, especially with other female attorneys. Since the members of my group were exceptionally skilled networkers and already had VPBODs, they all left the event with riches, including an international speaking engagement (with a nice fee and first-class accommodations), a writing opportunity, and new members for their VPBODs.

The greatest prize came after the event, when one of the group members arranged a meeting with a Professional Guru who was unable to attend the event but agreed to an airport breakfast just before her flight. The connection led to a job offer on another continent.

BOOKENDING

Bookending is the process of informing a supportive person when you begin and end a difficult task. It is an especially useful tool to address procrastination and fear. It is a powerful way of leveraging your board members.

The bookending mentoring modality is a low-maintenance method whereby your mentor can hold you accountable for your goals and give you the support you need in order to follow through, overcome procrastination, and do what you say you are going to do.

AN EXAMPLE OF BOOKENDING

Shira had been putting off completing her application for a very competitive coaching program. She was interested but had been unable to complete the application, mostly because of a hectic schedule coupled with a bit of fear and procrastination. As the deadline approached, she called her VPBOD Education Officer, Raul, who had been encouraging her to attend the program. During a brief call, Shira informed Raul that she would be working on the application and would call when she was finished. After the application was complete and ready for mailing, she texted him to let him know that she was headed for the post office. Bookending with board members offers you the advantage of their support and allows them to hold you accountable.

BOOKENDING WITH TWITTER

Today's technology enables us to bookend by phone, text message, e-mail, or online chat. Posting to Twitter.com offers writers immediate community and support using microblogging, posting short status updates in 140 characters or less.

MEETING-BEFORE-THE-MEETING

Denna, a female executive, came to me for executive coaching because her supervisors thought that she was not assertive enough. Her office team meetings had a traditional masculine culture: extremely competitive, lots of posturing for power, and filled with sports lingo. We discussed how being the only woman in a group of men had caused her to lose her voice. She had become what she described as "fuzzed over." Other terms I have heard for this are "de-skilled," "nonrational," and "loss of problem-solving facilities." Although she was always prepared, and sometimes even overprepared, she said very little at the actual meetings.

She began to use the method of the one-on-one **meeting-before-the-meeting**. She started to recognize her male counterparts' humanity—they were mates, fathers, and grandfathers. Most of all, she began to communicate information about her work and her ideas on joint projects and even shared a few personal details about herself. In the end, she got to know them as individuals and ultimately gained their respect.

The person with whom she experienced the most challenges eventually became one of her closest allies. One common interest that served to bridge the gaps in their relationship was that they were both cat lovers.

The meeting-before-the-meeting is not only a crucial, easy, and effective means of mentoring, but it is also a powerful technique for building professional relationships in general. The personal connections that are fostered by the meeting-before-the-meeting are not likely to happen at an official office meeting.

As a result of the discussions with her board members, Denna ultimately realized that success requires working effectively with colleagues (many in senior positions) whom we might find obnoxious. She learned that she did not have to like everyone, but she needed to establish and maintain successful working relationships with colleagues, and the meeting-before-the-meeting aided her in that process. Today Denna is a successful vice president and continues to use the meeting-before-the-meeting technique for herself and encourages it for her staff and mentees.

QUICK CHECK

A **quick check** is when a mentee contacts a board member quickly for one question that he or she will be able to answer easily because the board member knows the situation and knows you. Usually, a mentee needs a quick check when there is an urgent task at hand, such as when you are going for a job interview and you want to check in about a specific issue. Melody was a 26-year-old who was seeking a position for which she was qualified, but she was worried about a one-year gap in her résumé. She had already spent time with a board member preparing for the interview, and they had covered all potential questions—except the yearlong gap. She was concerned that the interviewer might think she was inconsistent or unreliable. So the morning of the interview, she reached out for a quick check to ask her board member, "What should I say about that yearlong gap that I spent backpacking through Europe?" In the quick check, the mentor could talk to her about how to bring it up, not wait for it to come up, to take charge of the issue and be proactive, so she wouldn't be thrown off balance when the interviewer brought it up. Had she not reached out for the quick check, she might have reacted defensively and sabotaged her interview. She was able to talk with the interviewer about the value that the year she spent traveling added to her skill set and her experience, and this turned a potential negative into a positive.

SPONSORING

A **sponsor** is someone with influence in your field who can expose you to others who can offer career guidance. Often, they see that you have promise and feel they can open doors to challenging assignments that you might not have been able to get on your own. In addition, sponsors will usually protect you from negative publicity and may help you with negotiating difficult situations with senior executives and other political tasks. Sponsors, more than any other mentor type, are most likely to help you to get a promotion or initiate an important introduction or connection that leads to a position that would have been completely out of your reach without the sponsor's assistance.

Sponsors are not necessarily people within your organization, but they often are. They are people who take you under their wings and cultivate your professional advancement. Finding sponsors and creating close relationships with them do not happen overnight. Most of the time, people sponsor those who are already succeeding and who remind them of themselves. Sponsors are publicly in support of you, so keep this in mind: if you screw up, you will be reflecting badly on your sponsors, and they will likely move away from the relationship. You can prevent mishaps by turning to your sponsors beforehand for help and assistance. Most often, they will be more than happy to offer you their wisdom and guidance.

A sponsor is your champion and greatest advocate. We will discuss sponsorship in more depth in Chapter 7. Sponsorship could be one of the most important mentoring modalities in terms of developmental assistance and career advancement. Your relationship with a sponsor should be one of mutual respect and admiration.

Having sponsors for each area of your professional life can be extremely helpful. Each sponsor will have unique qualities, abilities, and connections to assist you in achieving goals in your different career choices. Those in pursuit of a **boundaryless career** are more likely to need more sponsors in order to maximize the potential of accomplishing advancement in the varied fields they are pursuing.

A sponsor may be any one of the members of your Personal Board; he or she could be anyone from your CFO to your CTO to your **Diversity & Equity Officer**, depending on the focus of your career. However, sponsors most likely fall into the category of **Professional Guru** or Chairperson of the Board, simply because these are the two mentors on your board who have the most all-around knowledge. They are also more familiar with you and your aspirations and therefore can be of greater assistance. These are the officers you will be in contact with the most, so the development of a sponsoring relationship is more likely with them than with other board members. One of your tasks as the CEO of your VPBOD is to turn as many mentors into sponsors as possible.

FAMOUS MENTORING PAIRS: ENTERTAINMENT I—FILM AND TELEVISION

Mentor	Mentee
Warren Beatty, American film actor	Diane Keaton, American film actress
Ingmar Bergman, Swedish theater and film director	Woody Allen, American film writer and director
Peter Bogdanovich, American film director and writer	Cybill Shepherd, American TV and film actress
James L. Brooks, American TV and film director, producer, and writer	Cameron Crowe, American film director and writer
Johnny Carson, American TV comedian	Jay Leno, American TV comedian
John Cassavetes, American film actor and director	Martin Scorsese, American film director
Francis Ford Coppola, American film writer and director	George Lucas, American film writer and director
Bill Cosby, American TV and film actor and comedian	Sinbad, American TV actor and comedian
James Dean, American film actor	Dennis Hopper, American film actor
Adam Farrar, American film actor	Leonardo DiCaprio, American film actor
Jackie Gleason, American TV actor	Larry King, American talk-show host
Audrey Hepburn, British film actress	Elizabeth Taylor, British film actress
Stanley Kubrick, American film director and writer	Steven Spielberg, American film director and writer
Aaron Spelling, American film and TV producer	Darren Star, American TV producer and director
Mike Wallace, American journalist	Barbara Walters, American journalist and TV personality
Oprah Winfrey, American media mogul	Dr. Phil McGraw, American talk-show host

PROFILES IN MENTORSHIP: MAYA ANGELOU
AND OPRAH WINFREY

Oprah Winfrey refers to the mentorship of poet Maya Angelou as one of the most important relationships in her professional life (figure 2.1). The following quotes from Winfrey demonstrate the importance she placed on their relationship and also how significant Winfrey believes mentorship is in society today.

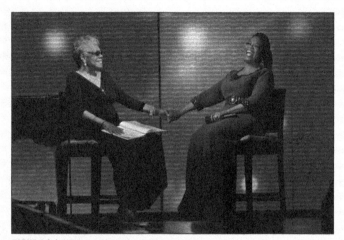

FIGURE 2.1 Mentor Maya Angelou, poet (left), with mentee Oprah Winfrey, TV host and journalist.

Most important lesson learned from Angelou:
"When you know better, you do better." (Maya Angelou)

Winfrey On the importance of Angelou's mentoring:
"When we met in Baltimore more than 20 years ago, our bond was immediate. We talked as if we had known each other our entire lives, and throughout my twenties and in the years beyond, Maya brought clarity to my life lessons. Now we have what I call a mother-sister-friend relationship. She's the woman who can share my triumphs, chide me with hard truths, and soothe me with words of comfort when I call her in my deepest pain" (Winfrey, 2000).

On the importance of mentorship:
"I think mentors are important and I don't think anybody makes it in the world without some form of mentorship. Nobody makes it alone. Nobody has made it alone. And we are all mentors to people even when we don't know it" ("An Interview with Oprah Winfrey," 2002).

On paying it forward

"I recognize that I serve as a mentor to many women. Because anybody who makes it, anybody who does achieve any level of success, that says to the rest of the world, 'This is possible.' That, to me, is the whole point of 'celebridom'; that's the whole point of fame, that's the whole point of notoriety—being able to take what fame you've been given, what notoriety, take what accomplishments, and use that in such a way that people say, 'This is possible.'" ("An Interview with Oprah Winfrey," 2002).

KNOWLEDGE NUGGETS

- The Virtual Personal Board of Directors methodology expands significantly on the traditional definition of mentoring relationships as dyadic (one-on-one), monogamous, and hierarchical.
- The VPBOD is a methodology one can employ in pursuit of the boundaryless career because of its versatility and accommodation of many different, distinct, and directed mentoring relationships.
- There are many types of mentors: boss-mentors, eMentors, group mentors, career coaches, inspirational mentors, family-member mentors, barrier-busting mentors, peer mentors, and situational mentors.
- The mentoring modalities that are most often employed in the VPBOD are reverse mentoring, invisible mentoring, one-minute mentoring, and sponsoring.

CHAPTER 3

INTRODUCING THE VIRTUAL PERSONAL BOARD OF DIRECTORS

> I've been blessed to find people who are smarter than I am, and they help me to execute the vision I have.
>
> Russell Simmons

So exactly what *is* a **Virtual Personal Board of Directors (VPBOD)**? According to *Fast Company* magazine, a Personal Board is a professional support network created to gain access to a vast pool of knowledge, resources, and expertise.

Its most outstanding and unique characteristic is that it is *virtual*, or exists only as a mental construct. Unlike with a traditional board of directors, VPBOD members are not required to attend in-person meetings, make formal commitments, agree to onerous obligations, or share in fundraising or fiduciary responsibilities. The members of your Personal Board do not necessarily know one another, and you need not extend a formal invitation for someone to join your board. Members' primary method of participating on your Personal Board is providing you with advice, information, and guidance when *you* seek them out and ask for it.

The major advantages of having a Personal Board include having access to the experience and wisdom of people normally not available to you for the purpose of providing advice regarding your career advancement. A Personal Board is a group of trusted and respected advisors, corresponding to specific aspects of your professional life. By leveraging the combined knowledge and expertise of a group of professional role models—specifically selected for their particular expertise and professional positions—you will be able to go further in your career and achieve more of your goals. You may think of your VPBOD as your own **professional posse**, a group of people on whom you can depend for unbiased, informed, and educated opinions on a variety of matters, ranging from professional (should I take that unexpected promotion?) to more personal (is now the right time to take an extended maternity leave?).

Scholars who specialize in the study of **developmental networks** and mentoring methodology recognize that multiple mentoring relationships are necessary. Higgins and Kram (2001) assert: "Individuals may need to draw on relationships from a variety of sources, not just senior-level, intra-organizational relationships for developmental assistance." Expanded mentoring networks that do not rely on a one-on-one model are expanding as the new millennium progresses, not only in the fields of mental health and psychotherapy but also in schools, civic and nonprofit organizations, and corporate settings. For example, Columbia University offers a "Responsible Conduct of Research" seminar, for the stated reason that "Mentoring is one of the primary means for one generation of scientists to impart their knowledge to succeeding generations" (Kalichman, 2001). Zerzan et al. (2009) states: "Effective mentoring is likely one of the most important determinants of success in academic medicine and research." In addition, in the field of medicine, the authors state: "Institutions may assign mentors, but often multiple mentors are helpful for specific needs, so a mentee may need to look for other mentors beyond those officially assigned."

Many successful businesses also include mentoring programs as part of their corporate culture in order to foster the development of these essential relationships in their own employees. This is because professionals who have access to the practical and emotional support of mentors perform better, are more satisfied in their positions, and develop advanced skill sets more quickly than those who do not have the guidance of a mentor. Corporations such as IBM employ mentoring programs for employee retention, education, and diversity outreach. According to DiversityInc.com, "The mentoring efforts of this huge multinational corporation whose focus is both consulting and technology, are world-class, with more than 80 percent of U.S. managers participating. A variety of mentoring programs, including virtual mentoring, are available to all employees" (Visconti, 2012).

The difference with the VPBOD is that you take it with you from job to job as you progress in your career. Rather than relying on your organization or institution for guidance in your mentoring needs, the VPBOD system encourages professionals—at all stages of their careers—to proactively take control of their mentoring needs and create and maintain a network of professionals with whom they can consult regarding all kinds of professional conundrums.

WHAT MAKES THE VPBOD DIFFERENT?

The VPBOD system differs from traditional mentorship models in many ways. Virtual Board members do not meet as a group and do not interact with one another. *You* are the nexus of your Virtual Board; the primary mentoring relationship exists only between each individual board member and the Chief Executive Officer (CEO)—*you*. A good metaphor for the structure and operation of a VPBOD is a wagon wheel. You can think of yourself as the hub and each board member as a spoke on the wheel. Although you are all moving together down the same road, you are at the center, and the spokes, or board members, revolve around you. And while each board member contributes valuable qualities to the smooth functioning of the wheel as a whole, each spoke is connected to you and only you. When all of your spokes are accounted for, your wheel will have more integrity and function more effectively. We'll continue with this metaphor in more detail in later chapters.

There are three defining characteristics of a VPBOD:

1. *It is virtual.* Your VPBOD is virtual. You will never hold formal meetings or gather as a group. The members will not be aware of one another or speak to one another. The VPBOD is a mental construct for the purpose of organizing and maintaining your professional developmental network. You can use the complementary app that corresponds to the VPBOD system, online at www. VirtualPersonalBoard.com, which provides an array of mentor management tools, including a contact directory.
2. *It is personal.* Your VPBOD is personal to you; the people on your board are individuals you collect throughout your everyday personal and professional interactions in order to help you meet your individual career goals. Your mentors may not even know that they are on your board.
3. *You choose your board.* A board of directors is a body made up of trusted advisors who assist the CEO in making important decisions about running the corporation. These elected or appointed members jointly oversee the activities of a company or organization. Here, you are the CEO, the corporation is your career, and you will be choosing the board members.

The VPBOD consists of 13 distinct offices, which are listed in the next section, and you will select and appoint mentors to staff those offices. We'll discuss this in more detail later.

THE OFFICES OF THE VPBOD

The VPBOD is characterized by a well-defined structure inspired by and based on corporate board structure. The VPBOD structure is simple, straightforward, and clear-cut. The VPBOD is made up of 13 offices; a short description of each office follows, and in-depth discussions are included in Chapter 4.

1. You are the *Chief Executive Officer (CEO)* of your VPBOD and the primary stakeholder in your professional success. The CEO of a Personal Board is in charge of recruiting all board members, making all decisions, and maintaining your board.
2. The office of *Chairperson of the Board* is held by your primary mentor, the person to whom you most often turn for advice with the most crucial career choices.
3. The *Professional Guru* is a colleague who works in the same field—or maybe even holds the same title—as you do, who will be able to provide answers for the

most detail-oriented questions and offer sage advice about complicated profession-specific questions.

4. The *Chief Technical Officer CTO* is someone who has specific technical expertise whom you can turn to for advice and information about technological topics.

5. The *Chief Financial Officer CFO* is someone who has specific experience with one or many different aspects of personal or business finance, such as taxes, money management, or investment.

6. The *Chief Political Analyst* is a person who has a particular aptitude for handling difficult or complex issues that are characterized by power and political dynamics in the organization or among colleagues.

7. The *Chief Legal* Advisor is an individual who is very knowledgeable about the law and legal matters. Your Chief Legal Advisor may or may not actually be an attorney but might just be someone who happens to know a lot about some aspect of the law.

8. The *Ethics & Morals (E&M) Officer* is someone known to have a strong sense of integrity and who adheres to a strict moral code. The E&M Officer is able to provide guidance regarding issues that require the perspective of a moral and principled individual.

9. The *Marketing & Branding (M&B) Officer* is a colleague who can assist you in developing and maintaining your personal brand, in addition to advising you regarding how to market yourself professionally.

10. The *Diversity & Equity (D&E) Officer*'s function is to offer advice on issues regarding organizational culture, potential bias, discrimination, and "identity politics" that impact your professional functioning. Your D&E Officer is able to provide you with an unbiased perspective on how you are perceived by others, offer insights that can help you navigate unintentional bias against you, or help you understand how you may be inadvertently alienating colleagues or managers. When necessary, your D&E Officer can advise you about how best to respond in the professional milieu when issues of subtle or overt discrimination based on gender, race, culture, or sexual orientation are interrupting your career. The D&E Officer will also address any privileged identities that you may hold, such as white, male, heterosexual, by helping you learn what you don't know about the impact of privilege and bias in professional settings.

11. The *Education Officer* is someone who has a passion for learning and will be a resource for figuring out how you can advance professionally by pursuing various educational opportunities, such as advanced degrees, training programs, or professional certifications.

12. The *Health & Wellness (H&W) Expert* is a person uniquely qualified to assist you with the management of your mental, physical, and spiritual health. The H&W Expert will be able to give you an impartial outside perspective on how your professional life and work habits may have negative and positive impacts on your health.

13. As your Personal Board develops, there may be a role for **Members-at-Large**, individuals who do not fall into one particular category at the current juncture,

although they may at some later point in time; these are considered "mentors-at-large" until or unless they are assigned to a particular office.

Each position has a specific function that relates to its corresponding area, and these correspondences are fairly obvious: the Chief Legal Advisor will perform the function of being a repository of legal information and legal advice. One unique feature of the Virtual Personal Board, which separates it from a traditional board, is that each office is not limited to being occupied by a single mentor. In fact, it should be your goal to staff each office with as many and as varied mentors as possible. You should do this for three reasons. First, this ensures that you have access to a variety of opinions, information, and experience that can only be available from an assemblage of mentors. Second, having multiple mentors fill each office is a type of insurance policy; in case of an emergency, such as a subpoena that requires your immediate response, you can be sure that *one* of the mentors on your Legal Advisory Board will be available for consultation. The third reason you should staff each office with multiple mentors is to ensure demographic variety in each of your offices, being sure to include different genders, races, sexual orientations, career levels, and age groups.

Some mentees may not require as much, or as in-depth, assistance in any of the areas that each board position corresponds to. For example, a computer programmer may not need as much technical assistance as an artist, so the office of the CTO may only consist of one mentor. However, as you begin the board-building process, the positions listed above represent the core stations to target for appointment. Start by reflecting on the specific career areas where you would benefit most from mentoring, and prioritize filling the associated board position. By filling every one of these roles, over time, you will create a well-rounded VPBOD that will serve you now and in the future. Detailed descriptions of the role and function of each of the offices of the VPBOD follows in Chapter 4.

THE COMPOSITION OF YOUR PERSONAL BOARD

Every person's board is different and therefore personal. Every well-rounded and productive VPBOD should consist of a wide range of types of mentors. You will personalize your board depending on the stage of your career, your current aspirations, and your particular profession. For example, if you are a young professional just starting out, you may want to make sure that you have a strong Chairperson who has many years of experience in your chosen field, so that you have a strong role model for comparison and inspiration as you craft your own career. On the other hand, if you are midway through your career and are transitioning to a position in executive management, you may want to ensure that you maintain relationships with younger professionals who are closer to the action, on the "front lines," so you don't lose touch with the trenches in your higher-level position in the hierarchy. The composition of your particular board may vary depending on your chosen field, your career level, and other factors.

ROLLING WITH YOUR PERSONAL BOARD

You can think of your board as a wheel on the wagon of your career. You are the hub of the wheel, and each spoke represents the various offices of the board. When your board is functioning smoothly, that is, when appropriate mentors are occupying each office of the board, then your wagon wheel—and your career—can roll along more smoothly. However, when one spoke is broken, missing, or misaligned, you'll have a bumpy ride. The more spokes that are faulty, the bumpier the ride will become.

Figure 3.1 illustrates how the wagon-wheel metaphor applies to the structure and function of your VPBOD. The wheel represents the board as a whole. You can think of it as a round table with the various board members sitting around it. The board is a circle of mentors arranged around you. You are represented by the center, or hub, of the wheel. This is because you are the center of the board and the one central element around which the wheel, representing your circle of mentors, revolves. Each spoke—or board office—connects the hub to the wheel. The spokes do not connect to one another, symbolizing the independent nature of each board members from one another. The common denominator in the Virtual Personal Board is you.

Just like an actual wagon wheel, your Personal Board requires constant maintenance. Spokes, or board member relationships, need to be maintained, repaired, or sometimes replaced completely. Likewise, the hub of the wheel—you—must be as strong and solid as possible so that all the spokes can function properly.

Above, each board member (as represented by a spoke of the wheel) is connected ONLY to you (the CEO) and NOT to each other. Your board members as a whole make up your Circle of Mentors, represented by the outer ring. However, your board will never meet as a group or consult with each other except in the situation that you make this happen for a particular reason.

FIGURE 3.1 The Virtual Personal Board of Directors as a wagon wheel.

SUBCOMMITTEES OF YOUR PERSONAL BOARD

At different points during your career, you may require more than just the consultation of a single board member. Just as a corporate board features various subcommittees, so does the VPBOD. Each subcommittee is an ad hoc assembly of various board members that you put together on the fly as you encounter issues with which you require a variety of opinions or would like to compare the advice of a number of different mentors.

Remember, one of the key aspects of the VPBOD is that it is *virtual*. While corporate board subcommittees meet in person to address the issue for which they have been assembled, the subcommittees of your VPBOD will not ever meet physically in a boardroom. Rather, the subcommittee is a mental construct for your own organizational purposes. As you work through an issue or problem and you decide to consult a subcommittee, you assemble board members in a virtual sense. You then consult each one separately and synthesize their opinions and advice. You do not call an actual meeting of all the board members selected for any given subcommittee; remember, you want to keep your mentors independent and separate from one another and only consult them one-on-one.

There are three main types of subcommittees that you will routinely assemble in leveraging your VPBOD:

1. Your *SWAT Team* is a subcommittee that you assemble when you have an urgent issue that requires immediate redress by means of consultation with two or more members of your Personal Board.
2. The *Executive Committee* is the group of people whose opinions you pool together when you have a crucial decision to make that requires multiple points of view.
3. The *Diversity & Equity (D&E) Committee* is assembled primarily to address issues regarding organizational culture, potential bias, discrimination, and "identity politics" that have an impact on your professional functioning. Your D&E Committee is made up of members from different demographic groups who can offer insight from perspectives that are different from your own.

We will delve more deeply into the subcommittee concept and its application in Chapter 7.

One of the most important principles to understand regarding the VPBOD is that it is a system that relies heavily on the integrity of its structure in order to function properly. Structural systems also cannot efficiently function if clear ground rules are not laid out and strictly adhered to. The **Rules of Engagement** are the top 17 rules governing the VPBOD methodology. Detailed explorations of each Rule of Engagement can be found throughout the book in the proper context, but they are summarized as follows:

THE RULES OF ENGAGEMENT FOR MENTEES

Rule 1. Don't keep score. Generosity is the key to successful networking and board development; always seek opportunities to be helpful.

Rule 2. Select two or three board members whom you want to change from mentors into sponsors. Develop a plan to deepen the relationships.

Rule 3. When meeting with board members or potential members, don't just ask questions. Share your thoughts, opinions, and feelings so they can get to know you.

Rule 4. Look for opportunities to collaborate with board members. Mentorship works best when both parties are getting their needs met.

Rule 5. Limit your requests of any one board member. The main goal is not to overwhelm one member by demanding too much of his or her time. Requests should be limited to a maximum of six hours a year.

Rule 6. Always offer to pay the tab. While the more senior board members may offer to put bills on their expense accounts, you should offer and should never suggest a place where you cannot afford to pay the bill.

Rule 7. Never "officially" ask anyone to be a member of your board; it is a mental construct for your use only, and making the arrangement official puts unnecessary pressure on your mentor.

Rule 8. Avoid inviting mentors to purely social events that you consider as part of your personal life. Interacting with board members in nonprofessional environments will most likely be awkward and unproductive in terms of the main purpose of your relationship: advancing your career.

Rule 9. Gift your board member with your support. Gifting does not necessarily involve a physical item; you can gift your mentors by zealously supporting their endeavors, sharing your special talents with them, or simply offering your time.

Rule 10. Keep in contact with your board members via social media such as websites. Subscribe to their blogs, follow them on Twitter, and connect with them on LinkedIn.

Rule 11. Always blind-copy all your board members when sending group e-mails. When sending a group e-mail, never expose board members' e-mail addresses.

Rule 12. *Keep your mentors' upcoming special events on your calendar, such as a major speaking engagement or TV appearance, so that you can acknowledge them or check to see how things went with a quick e-mail or text.*

Rule 13. Write up a "Year in Review" letter or e-mail for all of your board members annually. Draw up a standardized boilerplate letter that summarizes the activities and progress you made over the preceding year, with an emphasis on important accomplishments or awards and recognition.

Rule 14. *Keep in touch with your board members on a regular basis with issues that are important to them. Sending your board members periodic updates about your activities or achievements will keep you on their radar. Just don't bombard them with too much e-mail. Save these for special accomplishments.*

Rule 15. Develop a schedule to connect with your board members over teas, lunches, or drinks. Keep a record to remind you of your board-nurturing activities.

Rule 16. Develop a tradition, such as an annual lunch with your Chairperson, Professional Guru, or members you are seeking to convert from mentor to sponsor.

Rule 17. Plan at least two to three months in advance to connect with board members at your industry's annual event. When you register for the event, reach out to board members to secure time with them. A professional conference is a rare opportunity to enjoy face-to-face time and deepen your relationship.

FAMOUS MENTORING PAIRS: POLITICS I

Mentor	Mentee
Zbigniew Brzezinski, US national security advisor	Madeleine Albright, first female US secretary of state
George H. W. Bush, US presidentSir Hugh Casson, architect and illustrator	James Baker, US secretary of stateCharles, prince of Wales
Alfonse D'Amato, US senator	George E. Pataki, governor of New York
William Fulbright, US senator	Bill Clinton, US president
Al Gore, US vice president	Joe Lieberman, US senator
Thomas Jefferson, US president	Meriwether Lewis, explorer
Sir Keith Joseph, British barrister and politician	Margaret Thatcher, first female UK prime minister
Richard Nixon, US president	George W. Bush, US president
Georges Pompidou, French president	François Mitterrand, French president
Yitzhak Rabin, Israeli prime minister	Ehud Barak, Israeli minister of defense
Ronald Reagan, US president	Christine Todd Whitman, first female governor of New Jersey
Theodore Roosevelt, US president	William Howard Taft, US president
George Wythe, jurist and legal scholar	Thomas Jefferson, US president

PROFILES IN MENTORSHIP: WHO MENTORED PRESIDENT BILL CLINTON?

William Jefferson Clinton, the 42nd president of the United States, discusses the importance of mentorship in both his professional and his personal life, and he describes how mentors helped him achieve his dreams and aspirations.

On the importance of having a mentor as your champion:
"My high school band director, Virgil Spurlin, had a huge impact on my life. He thought that everybody was good at something and if he just looked hard enough he could find it, he could convince them of it, and he could raise their aspirations and their hopes. He was unbelievable. All my life I thought of him. I stayed in touch with him on and off until he passed away. I really felt that my early years with him convinced me that I could organize and run things. That I could do whatever I wanted to do and that I could actually marshal other people in a common effort, and, of course, if you're in politics that's very important."

On mothers as mentors:
"I think the example of my mother helped me a lot. . . she told me repeatedly that every day was a gift, and that obstacles were as much a part of life as opportunities, and you just had to go on. And I had this sort of dogged endurance throughout my life."

On mentors as role models:
"Sometimes your parents or other mentors can have a big impact just by the way they are with you and with other people, by what you see about the way they live, whether they are with you all the time, or what words come out of their mouth."

KNOWLEDGE NUGGETS

- A Virtual Personal Board of Directors is a group of trusted and respected advisors from various parts of your life.
- You will be able to advance your career further and achieve more of your goals than would be possible without a Personal Board.
- When choosing the positions of your board members, it is important to keep in mind that you want to select members who have skills, experience, and knowledge that you may be lacking.

- By arranging your VPBOD members into a number of subcommittees—SWAT Team, Executive Committee, Diversity & Equity Committee—you will be able to maximize the efficiency with which you can access their guidance.
- The most important times when the advice of a trusted board member could improve and inform your decision-making process involve job-related decisions, ethical issues, personal decisions, referrals and information, and expert opinions.
- You should be on the look-out for potential additions to your VPBOD everywhere you go, even in social situations and in your personal life.

CHAPTER 4

THE BOARD IN FOCUS

Surround yourself with only people who are going to lift you higher.

Oprah Winfrey

THE POSITIONS ON THE BOARD

The most important conceptual—and structural—component of the Virtual Personal Board of Directors (VPBOD) is the board member. Like a traditional board of directors, the structure of the VPBOD is made up of approximately one dozen offices, or positions, such as CEO, CFO, and Chairperson of the Board. Each office pertains to a specific function, and each board member plays a discrete role as the go-to person regarding all matters related to his or her field of expertise. According to Lois Zachary in *The Mentee's Guide*: "The board has the advantage of providing multiple perspectives and diverse feedback to a mentee by clarifying, pushing, and expanding the mentee's thinking, promoting personal reflection, and functioning as a sounding board" (Zachary, 2009, p. 10).

Although there are similarities between the functioning of a mentoring VPBOD and a traditional corporate board of directors, there are more significant differences. Unlike on a traditional board, it is you, as CEO—and not the board members—who are responsible for all final decisions. The VPBOD does not make decisions by committee. The mentoring VPBOD functions much like a board of advisors: the CEO takes all opinions into consideration, synthesizes them, and makes his or her own decision.

Your VPBOD is made up of 12 positions; however, ultimately, you should aim to staff each office with multiple mentors adept in that particular area. For example, a developed VPBOD may feature six Legal Advisors, four Technical Officers, and five Ethics & Morals Officers. Each department of your Personal Board will have multiple mentors for two reasons: first, in order for you to have access to a diversity of opinions in any given area and, second, to ensure that you have access to an expert in any given field at any given moment in time.

In addition to diversifying the range of expertise on your board and ensuring round-the-clock availability, it is also helpful to arrange the various mentors in each office of your Personal Board into "strings." This functionality is similar to a football roster—a team has a first-string quarterback, a second-string quarterback, and so on. Likewise, you'll strategically arrange the mentors staffing each position of your Personal Board into a first string, a second string, a third string, and so on. The go-to board member—the advisor to whom you turn first—is considered your first string. However, if he or she is unavailable, you are not at a standstill; you have the option of tapping your second string as a backup. Each office of the board—from the Chairperson to the Education Officer—should include multiple mentors, strategically classified in levels according to the importance of their opinions, their availability, and a variety of other factors that we will explore in more depth in later chapters.

For example, if your first-string CTO does not have the resources, information, or time to assist you with a particular issue, keeping backup Technical Officers on the second, third, fourth, and even fifth strings will ensure that you will *always* have someone to turn to when you need advice. Therefore, this component of the VPBOD system will enhance your decision-making process by enabling you to synthesize and evaluate a range of opinions and perspectives when making vital decisions. Maintaining a roster of Technical Officers empowers you to leverage your pool of technical resources as efficiently and effectively as possible.

As your career progresses, your board will grow and evolve, and you may need to move a second-string board member up to occupy the first string. By maintaining such depth in your board positions, you ensure that you can customize the positions to your particular needs as you mature, develop, and progress over the course of your career. Since membership is fluid, you do not have to worry about having definite, steadfast positions for each and every mentor on your board at all times. All members can play multiple roles; as you get to know them, you will learn their full array of talents, and some mentors may become more useful to you in different roles from those you originally intended them to take. There are no limits to the roles your board members may play. You can keep some individuals on the warm-up bench for the appropriate time when you need more routine access to their specific knowledge, experience, and expertise.

What follows in this chapter are in-depth descriptions of the positions that make up a mentoring VPBOD. Familiarize yourself with the Virtual Personal Board structure and the functions of each position. Each board office description is accompanied by examples of that position in action to illustrate how one may leverage a Virtual Personal Board for maximum personal and professional growth. These examples draw on my own experiences with mentees and coaching clients and on my experience building and maintaining my own Personal Board over the course of my 30-year career.

Once you know your way around the general Personal Board structure and positions, we will explore your goals and ambitions in depth. Once you have clarified your own objectives for the future, you can design a customized Personal Board that fulfills the requirements unique to your individualized professional aspirations. As you review the following board descriptions, keep in mind that you will soon be selecting multiple mentors for each of these positions. As you read through each position described in this chapter, jot down the names of individuals you might consider appointing to your Personal Board in the worksheets provided at the end of each section. We will come back to these initial brainstorms in later chapters.

> Change is inevitable. Progress is optional.
>
> Walt Disney

CHIEF EXECUTIVE OFFICER

You are the Chief Executive Officer (CEO) of your Virtual Personal Board of Directors. In keeping with the board of directors metaphor, as the CEO of your board, it is your responsibility to choose the members, synthesize their input, and draw on their resources and contributions as needed. *You* are in control of your VPBOD, so choosing and appointing members is your sole responsibility. However, because it is a virtual board, you may move members around as you see fit—*without* discussions or consultations—as your career demands. And as the CEO, your choices are never subject to a vote or referendum: you are the sole individual who will draw on the resources of your individual Personal Board.

When choosing the relative positions on your board roster, it is important to keep in mind that you want to select members who have skills, experience, and knowledge that you may be lacking. In addition, you should appoint members who are both similar and different from you, in terms of job title and demographic traits such as age, culture, race, socioeconomic status, sexual orientation, and gender. This is important, because you want to solicit advice from individuals with a different point of view, in addition to comparing notes with colleagues who have experiences similar to your own.

Remember that you are only using your board members as *advisors* on their various specialties. It is up to you to do the necessary research and work both before and after consulting them; preparation will ensure that you do not waste the time of busy professionals. Rather, you should cull specific wisdom from them bit by bit at the appropriate moments in order to maximize the efficiency of your relationships with board members. If you find yourself needing more than five or six hours of consultation over the course of a year from a specific board member, you might consider hiring a professional career coach or therapist to assist you with that aspect with your professional development. Don't rely too heavily on board members for your day-to-day career-development needs. If you do, you will become a drain on their time and energy, and they may withdraw from your relationship, making it impossible to maintain them as functioning members of your Personal Board.

WORKSHEET: PEOPLE I ADMIRE

Think of five people whom you admire and whose personalities you are drawn to.
List their names and their standout qualities below, as potential role models for
how you may envision yourself in the future.

Name   Qualities

_____   _____

_____   _____

_____   _____

_____   _____

_____   _____

CHAIRPERSONS OF THE BOARD

This is the position of your primary mentors—the people to whom you turn with the crucial career issues, those whose perspectives you most value. Chairpersons of the Board are professionals whom you respect, admire, and wish to emulate. They are role models who inspire your own vision of your future "best self," whom you can model your own career after. Your Chairpersons may not necessarily occupy these key roles throughout your career; as you develop and expand, you may outgrow a Chairperson and require a new one to meet your changing needs.

The Chairpersons should display a similar professional temperament to your own. Chairpersons are those with whom you enjoy an authentic relationship; they know your professional goals and can therefore provide qualified advice appropriate to your circumstances. Your chairpersons should be privy to the "real you," in order to be able to guide you down the right path. They must know your deepest fears, your highest hopes, and your most daring dreams. Do not put up a front with your Chairpersons—or with any of the members of your Personal Board. If you do so, you are wasting both your time *and* theirs, because mentors cannot provide proper advice or guidance to a person they do not actually *know*.

You do not necessarily need to share a career track or professional title in common with your Chairpersons, although you may. What is most important for this mentoring relationship is that they are genuinely invested in you as a person and know you well enough to provide emotional support and career advice specifically tailored for you as an individual.

WORKSHEET: POSSIBLE CHAIRPERSONS FOR
MY PERSONAL BOARD

Name   Relationship

_____   _____

_____   _____

_____   _____

_____   _____

_____   _____

PROFESSIONAL GURUS

These are individuals who work in your particular field, preferably holding the title you ultimately aspire to achieve. Your Professional Gurus should have a wealth of experience and should have achieved major success in their field. These board members will be able to answer in-depth questions specific to your chosen career. They are nuts-and-bolts experts who know the ins and outs of your particular job and your industry in general. Having Professional Gurus on your board is invaluable for a mentee who needs someone who can answer technical questions about the details of your job responsibilities and for access to insider information about the field. The Professional Gurus and your Chairpersons are the board members you should consult when considering major career-changing decisions that will irrevocably affect your professional life.

How do you identify a Professional Guru to consider for your Personal Board? Potential Professional Gurus display many, if not all, of the following characteristics:

- They have thorough knowledge about their field.
- They are go-to people when it comes to questions and information about the profession.
- They are influential thought leaders, who shape the conversation in their field.
- They are visionary dreamers, who have innovative, thought-provoking ideas.
- They want their work to have an impact on the future of the profession and are concerned with leaving a legacy for future generations.
- They have massive influence, both within their profession and in general.
- They have a big-picture perspective when it comes to overall trends in the profession and the industry.
- They are popular, well-known individuals; everyone in the field knows who they are.
- They are optimists, who espouse idealistic perspectives and maintain a never-say-die attitude.
- They are **connectors**, who can bring different people from every corner of the profession together.
- They are open and receptive and enjoy mentoring younger colleagues in addition to peers.
- They have written extensively about the field and are usually sought-after speakers on the lecture circuit.
- They are often activists devoted to achieving a mission or accomplishing a lifelong goal in their field.

Such dynamic and influential individuals are constantly in high demand by colleagues. They usually have a long list of current and potential mentees vying for their attention. So how can you make yourself stand out in the eyes of Professional Gurus?

Here are a few ways you may distinguish yourself in order to cultivate mentoring relationships with potential Professional Gurus:

- Engage them by seeking advice about a specific professional goal in which they may be particularly interested.
- They need researchers, co-presenters, and co-writers, so volunteer to collaborate with them and contribute to their work.
- They need people to whom to refer their current mentees and sponsees for peer connections, so make yourself available to assist them in this regard.
- Take classes or workshops they may be teaching in order to absorb and learn all the knowledge they have to offer.
- Become the exact resource they are looking for in any capacity possible, especially in terms of carrying on their legacy.
- Communicate with them via social networks such as LinkedIn and Facebook and also in more personal ways such as via letters and e-mail.
- Research and become knowledgeable about issues they care about so you can engage them in intelligent dialogue about these subjects.
- Become familiar with their particular interests so that you can provide them with practical support.

If you find potential Professional Gurus you would like on your Personal Board, know that you may not be able to attract their attention immediately. Do not be discouraged if you do not seem to interest them right away. In the meantime, follow their careers, and keep tabs on their professional activities. Until you make one-on-one contact with them, appoint them to your Personal Board as invisible mentors. Follow them on blogs, lectures, TED talks, and YouTube videos.

Remember, every guru wants a protégé—someone who can carry his or her message and legacy into the future. Your goal is to find Professional Gurus for whom you can be a guru-in-training. The right gurus for your Personal Board will be those who can see themselves in you and will therefore take a personal interest in your professional development. Keep in mind that your Personal Board is virtual—meaning that no explicit invitation to serve on your board is required for you to enjoy the benefits of a mentoring relationship with a Professional Guru. Once you cultivate a meaningful relationship with a Professional Guru, the ultimate goal is to have him or her act as your sponsor, leverage their influence to open doors, and introduce you to colleagues that can help you advance professionally.

WORKSHEET: POSSIBLE PROFESSIONAL GURUS
FOR MY PERSONAL BOARD

Name   Relationship

_____   _____

_____   _____

_____   _____

_____   _____

_____   _____

THE BOARD IN FOCUS: CHAIRPERSONS VS. PROFESSIONAL GURUS

The Chairpersons of the Board are those who have a lot of admirable qualities; they are all-around superstars in multiple ways, from political savvy to professional expertise to superb communication skills. The Chairpersons of your board help you analyze general professional issues rather than assessing the detail-oriented nuts and bolts of your field. They have a sense of the big picture in terms of the corporate landscape and about who you are as both an individual and a professional. Your Chairpersons should have an intuitive sense of what is going on in your life, on both a personal and a professional level, in order to advise you most constructively. You and your Chairpersons must enjoy a natural rapport and mutual respect.

The Chairpersons of your board head your cheerleading squad; they reassure you and remind you of your true value. They can help you to devise strategies to ensure that you receive monetary compensation commensurate with your skills and level of expertise. You should turn to your Chairpersons when negotiating a promotion and evaluating new job offers. The Chairpersons also keep you up-to-date on trends in your profession and, in light of current trends, assess your skills and recommend when to enhance or expand on them. The Chairpersons are a valuable resource when it comes to finessing relationships and political quandaries at the workplace.

Your Chairpersons can also help you hone your vision for the long-term trajectory of your career and assist in devising goals and choosing the next steps on the road to your ultimate aspirations. Your Chairpersons are also the primary mentors for building your board by connecting you with key players in your organization and in your field and may invite you to industry events that heighten your professional profile.

You and your Chairpersons do not need to have identical job titles. You should, on the other hand, seek Professional Gurus who hold your current title or the most advanced title on your career track. The Professional Gurus are just as significant as your Chairpersons but play a vastly different role. Your Professional Guru should be detail-oriented, seasoned professionals with a backward-and-forward understanding of your specific profession, rooted in years of experience.

Professional Gurus are likely to be more involved with the internal, nuts-and-bolts aspects rather than the external, big-picture attributes of a particular field. The Professional Gurus are your go-to advisors when you absolutely need the most knowledgeable expert available to answer your question or offer advice. Unlike with the Chairpersons, it is not important that your Professional Gurus be intimately aware of the intricacies of your personal life. You tap the resource of your Professional Gurus when you need highly specialized and hard-to-come-by knowledge nuggets that come with decades of dedication to a profession. An individual who has achieved guru status in his or her field is most likely extremely busy and in high demand by colleagues and mentees. Turn to your Professional Gurus only when you need well-informed advice about the nitty-gritty details of a professional conundrum *and* you are completely prepared for the consultation.

CHIEF TECHNICAL OFFICERS

Chief Technical Officers (CTOs) are the mentors with whom you consult when you require technical or technological guidance. If you are tech-savvy yourself, you may not need extremely prominent CTOs or a very deep roster. However, with the crucial role the Internet plays in today's business world, almost everyone needs some help designing a website or establishing a social media presence—no matter what stage you are at in your career. Your CTOs should be knowledgeable about a range of technical areas, including not only the Internet but also communications in general and computer hardware and software. Your CTOs will be your go-to mentors when you need answers or advice, but more important, they should also be well connected to other techies to whom they can refer you. So don't choose that shy, withdrawn IT guy you met at your first job just because he is approachable; you want to make sure the CTOs of your board enjoy a broad network of all kinds of technical professionals that they can turn to for more detailed information—and to whom they can introduce you when it is time to expand the CTO area of your board with more specialized technical experts.

CTOs advise you how to best leverage the Internet for your professional growth in general. The specific types of activities your CTOs may assist you with or advise you about are many, including, but not limited to, strategizing the establishment of your Web presence, networking through blogging and social media, explaining the roles of networking sites such as LinkedIn for participating in online peer groups, suggesting a computer class you could take to improve your skills, and recommending computer equipment to increase your efficiency and productivity.

For example, one of my coaching clients, Amanda, age 37, turned to her CTO, Stuart, 26, when she found her psychotherapy practice floundering. This was not because of a lack of patients but was a result of organizational and managerial inefficiency. When she asked her CTO for his assessment on how she could streamline the administrative aspects of her practice, he advised her to purchase and install a new cutting-edge software program (something she had never heard of, much less considered using). Stuart then helped her install it on her laptop and on the office computer network. He gave her a brief tutorial on how to use it and referred her to a class where she could learn its more advanced functionality. This software program was specialized for psychotherapists in private practice and enabled Amanda to organize her case notes in an easily accessible and user-friendly format. This facilitated access to insurance companies and professional colleagues—such as her administrative assistant, practicing partner, and bookkeeper. The advice of her CTO helped to turn Amanda's once-floundering practice into a thriving, well-run small business. This ultimately boosted her self-confidence and also freed up so much time that she was able to expand her practice. Upon the insightful recommendation of Stuart, Amanda also began offering Skype sessions to long-distance clients whom she had turned away. With the extra time and peace of mind that a well-organized business afforded her, she was able to significantly increase her income thanks to the mentoring of her CTO.

WORKSHEET: POSSIBLE CHIEF TECHNICAL OFFICERS
FOR MY PERSONAL BOARD

Name   Relationship

_____   _____

_____   _____

_____   _____

_____   _____

_____   _____

CHIEF FINANCIAL OFFICERS

These are the people to whom you will turn when you have questions about finances—anything from what you should charge a client for a session to what kind of salary increase to request when offered a major promotion. Chief Financial Officers (CFOs) provide guidance on such issues as your compensation, benefits, retirement planning, disability, life insurance, capital investment in an expanding business, loads, mortgages, taxes, expense accounts, and more. Additionally, your CFOs may help you evaluate job offers, calculate asking rates for services, and give you an independent and well-informed perspective when sizing up job offers or promotions, specifically in terms of salary and other benefits such as flextime. The ideal CFOs have proven track records when it comes to managing money and a realistic view of finances. Many professionals, both young and more seasoned, are uncomfortable navigating financial issues. CFOs can recommend ways to diversify your income, no matter the stage of your career, and direct you to new ways of making money. This will enable you to become a more independent professional.

For example, Jennifer, a drug counselor at a large addiction treatment facility, was under consideration for a major promotion to a directorship. Jennifer was about to go on her second interview without even considering how much additional compensation she would request for the increased responsibilities of this new supervisory position. After consulting with Eileen, a seasoned CFO of a nonprofit organization much like her own, Jennifer learned that other employees at the director level were making significantly more than she had previously assumed. By consulting her CFO, Jennifer realized she was about to ask for $25,000 less than the average director salary. In addition, Eileen suggested that Jennifer ask for other benefits, such as the ability to work from home, traveling to conferences, representing the organization at industry events, and even tuition reimbursement for continuing education in management, budgeting, and coaching. Much to her disbelief, Jennifer was able to get these perks added to the compensation package for the directorship simply by asking for them. A consultation with her CFO enabled Jennifer to get the most out of this career move. Keep this in mind when considering accepting a job offer or negotiating a promotion: you could be costing yourself significant benefits and money by *not* consulting a CFO for guidance.

WORKSHEET: POSSIBLE CHIEF FINANCIAL OFFICERS
FOR MY PERSONAL BOARD

Name   Relationship

_____   _____

_____   _____

_____   _____

_____   _____

_____   _____

CHIEF POLITICAL ANALYSTS

Chief Political Analysts are successful, professionals with specific knowledge about navigating the murky and difficult waters of office politics. Good candidates are socially savvy and knowledgeable about the history of your organization and industry in general. Chief Political Analysts can provide invaluable guidance when you are walking a tightrope on the job, especially in adversarial situations in which feuding colleagues are pressuring you to choose sides or are causing conflict with your boss, higher-ups, or team members.

Although office politics is not a topic usually covered by educational or training programs, it is a very important factor in determining your professional success or failure. Learning office politics on the job can be extremely costly, so having Chief Political Analysts to whom you can turn for guidance regarding interdepartmental tension, personality conflicts, the office rumor mill, and similar matters will prove to be invaluable. The Chief Political Analysts' advice will prevent you from making detrimental mistakes that could potentially cost you a pending promotion, a more prestigious position, or even your current position.

For example, Ronald, 42, a caseworker at an assisted living facility for the past 10 years, was nervous about a major shake-up in upper management. For the past six months, many mid-level directors and supervisors—including Ronald's direct supervisor—had been replaced, and Ronald was understandably concerned that he was next. Most of Ronald's colleagues at the facility assumed that the firings were the work of the newly hired CEO, Josh. The new boss had quickly earned a reputation for being intimidating, insensitive, and judgmental. When Josh reached out to Ronald to see if he was interested in being considered for a higher position reporting directly to him, Ronald was surprised at how friendly and approachable the new CEO was at their meeting. Although Ronald was eager for advancement and a supervisory role, he was worried that accepting would alienate close colleagues in the office, who all seemed to be aligned against Josh.

Ronald turned to a Chief Political Analyst on his Personal Board for her opinion on how to accept the new position while maintaining good relationships with his coworkers. His Chief Political Analyst, Marjorie, his former supervisor, had retired. Since she was not a part of the organization and had no investment in the decision, she was able to offer an unbiased opinion. In addition, Marjorie knew many of the people involved and had insights into why many of Ronald's colleagues felt negatively about the new CEO.

Marjorie evaluated the situation and reassured Ronald that he need not worry about the opinions of his coworkers regarding Josh. She reasoned that the general resentment against him was fear about job security. Marjorie advised Ronald to accept Josh's job offer, reasoning that the risk of becoming alienated from colleagues was worth the reward of career advancement. Marjorie also advised Ronald that although his new position of authority would change the nature of his colleague relationships, he still needed to foster a sense of camaraderie and fellowship with them because of the importance of workplace alliances and collaboration.

WORKSHEET: POSSIBLE CHIEF POLITICAL OFFICERS
FOR MY PERSONAL BOARD

Name   Relationship

_____   _____

_____   _____

_____   _____

_____   _____

_____   _____

CHIEF LEGAL ADVISORS

Chief Legal Advisors (CLAs) are mentors who will assist you in protecting yourself in professional ventures, either as an entrepreneur or as an employee. You should have a team of Legal Advisors who are knowledgeable in matters relating to intellectual property, severance, termination, contract negotiation, and other matters that require seasoned professionals who are acquainted with the plethora of legal implications that inevitably arise over the course of your professional undertakings. You should always vet crucial career choices through your Legal Advisors before you commit; they may be able to highlight unforeseen ramifications of your decisions that may not even occur to you. Appointing practicing attorneys to your Personal Board is, of course, ideal; however, your Legal Advisors may simply be a collection of respected colleagues who are well versed in the legal aspects of your field and your profession.

Cheryl, age 30, was an early-childhood educator working at a charter school. For the last four years, she had been developing a program to help children suffering from the loss of a parent or siblings. Cheryl created a protocol and curriculum, which she first conducted while on staff. Upon encountering positive feedback and good results from her protocol, Cheryl began implementing the program at a number of other schools as a consultant with her organization's permission.

The great success of her program inspired Cheryl to leave her job and pursue a consultancy on a full-time basis. However, Cheryl was informed by her organization that she did not have the legal right to use the protocol or the curriculum after her resignation, despite the fact that she was its sole creator and that her name was associated with it.

Cheryl had a choice to make: stay on as a staff teacher or start her own consultancy business *without* the very successful childhood loss treatment program as a part of her service offerings. Cheryl had always been a cautious person, and starting her business without the childhood loss program made staying in her safe position even more appealing. However, before making a final decision, Cheryl consulted with Bryan, one of her CLAs. Bryan was her first-string mentor on this subject because Cheryl knew that he owned a small accounting business as his side hustle in addition to his full-time role as a corporate VP at a midsize estate-planning law firm. He helped her to brainstorm the pros and cons of remaining in her current role or taking the risk of starting her own company.

In addition to helping Cheryl to express her passion and fear about the potential of starting her own business, Bryan connected her to his attorney, who had been instrumental in helping him to set up his accounting business. Bryan's consultation followed the model outlined by Hoffman and Casnocha (2012) in *The Start-Up of You*, where they described the value of ABZ planning:

Plan A: Assess what you are doing now.
Plan B: What you pivot to when plan A is not working for you.
Plan Z: A lifeboat if all else fails.

ABZ planning is about being "flexibly persistent: always ready to adapt, but also persistent in driving towards set goals." Because the world changes so frequently, it's important to be flexible and plan accordingly.

Pivoting is when you shift your goals based on your gained knowledge. You do not pivot by shifting goals alone. You should pivot to take advantage of an opportunity or to avoid a shortcoming. Your opportunities should be ahead of the industry's trends.

Despite her trepidations, Cheryl was open and interested in pursuing this unexpected opportunity. Her meeting with Bryan helped her to gain focus on her growing displeasure with the limits and restrictions of her current position, even though she remained dedicated to her work with grieving children. As a result of their brainstorming session, Cheryl was able to create both a plan B and a plan Z fallback. Crafting these plans freed her to take a strategic risk and resign from her teaching position to pursue the dream of owning a consulting firm. Eighteen months later, Cheryl's consulting business is thriving and has required her to hire two other teacher-trainers to assist with her consultations.

This example demonstrates the importance of having access to a well-informed Chief Legal Advisor. Had Cheryl not sought the advice of her board, she may have languished in her restrictive institutional role.

WORKSHEET: POSSIBLE CHIEF LEGAL ADVISORS FOR MY PERSONAL BOARD

Name   Relationship

_____   _____

_____   _____

_____   _____

_____   _____

_____   _____

ETHICS & MORALS OFFICERS

The Ethics & Morals (E&M) Officers are important positions on your Personal Board. These individuals provide guidance regarding matters of judgment, principles, and values. One must adhere to a strict code of personal values no matter what one's profession. In order to keep yourself honest, it is imperative that you appoint E&M Officers with a reputation for maintaining the highest moral standards in your field.

There are countless situations in which the insightful advice of intuitive E&M Officers will prove invaluable. There are situations where ethical boundaries are nebulous, and you will need the outside perspective of E&M Officers in order to discriminate among the shades of gray that cause otherwise honest people to get in trouble. For example, during an unscheduled audit, missing session notes may come to light, and your supervisor may request that you backdate or otherwise falsify session notes to avoid penalties or loss of funding. When an opening for an administrative assistant comes up, a human resources director might be pressured by a VP to hire her niece who can't land a job, even though a dedicated intern about to graduate from college is slated to fill the position. What if a mentee asks you to affirm with a reference that she is experienced with a software program she does not yet know so she can land a coveted position? What do you do? E&M Officers can advise you in such quandaries. Your E&M Officers should have impeccable standards and be above reproach, perhaps past colleagues whom you admire for their integrity.

Phyllis was a 34-year-old social worker at a public hospital. One of her male colleagues, John, 43, a director of facilities, was written up for bullying. Although Phyllis currently enjoyed a pleasant camaraderie with John, it wasn't always that way. Eight years earlier, when she was first hired straight out of college, Phyllis did experience less than professional treatment by John. Phyllis attributed her previous issues with John to her own inability to stand up to him, in addition to his domineering, intimidating demeanor. Despite the fact that his behavior was completely inappropriate and unprofessional—he would make fun of her slight lisp, berate her for small mistakes, and play practical jokes at her expense—Phyllis never reported him. Instead, as she developed more confidence, she asserted herself and confronted him directly for his unacceptable behavior.

Merely threatening to report him to superiors proved to be an effective means of addressing and remedying John's problematic behavior—but only with respect to Phyllis. Even though John hadn't bullied Phyllis for several years, she was aware that he continued behaving inappropriately with other hospital employees, particularly young, female recent hires who were easily intimidated and too insecure to report him.

However, the time arrived when two young professionals did report John to HR for bullying. The hospital took bullying very seriously, and John could be dismissed for cause if an internal investigation found him guilty of the charges. John approached Phyllis about speaking on his behalf with the HR mediator. Despite the fact that Phyllis was well aware of his past unprofessional behavior, she had grown to genuinely like him over the years. To complicate matters, the two accusers, who knew about Phyllis's past run-ins with John, asked Phyllis to testify on *their* behalf by relating her previously unreported confrontations with John to the mediator.

Phyllis was paralyzed by the situation; she was not sure if she should advocate for John, support the two young women, or remain neutral. For advice, she turned to her E&M Officer, Alma, a former HR director of the hospital. Phyllis had been impressed by Alma's workshops on workplace harassment and professional etiquette. Alma now reminded Phyllis of how important it was to maintain a healthy balance between personal friendships and professional responsibilities. She encouraged Phyllis to prioritize maintaining her sense of integrity over any loyalty to John. Alma also advised her that the appropriate, ethical choice was to testify truthfully at the HR mediation.

When asked to testify, Phyllis did indeed share her previous experiences with John's bullying tendencies. However, she emphasized the fact that these altercations had stopped some years ago and made sure also to highlight John's positive qualities. As a result of Phyllis's testimony, hospital management did formally reprimand John for inappropriate behavior. He was put on a six-month probation and required to attend a weekly sensitivity-training workshop. By taking the moral high road as Alma's advised, Phyllis was able to preserve her friendship with John *and* her sense of integrity. Phyllis made the moral choice—despite her fear that testifying truthfully would result in catastrophic consequences for John—thanks to the emotional support and encouragement of Alma, her E&M Officer.

WORKSHEET: POSSIBLE ETHICS & MORALS OFFICERS
FOR MY PERSONAL BOARD

Name   Relationship

_____   _____

_____   _____

_____   _____

_____   _____

_____   _____

MARKETING & BRANDING OFFICERS

In today's business world, brands and logos are not just for big corporations. With the advent of social media and Internet marketing, every professional must give serious consideration to his or her personal brand. The Marketing & Branding (M&B) Officers are a crucial resource for developing and maintaining your personal brand. In order to distinguish yourself from the competition, stand out in the crowd, and make yourself memorable to colleagues and customers, you should employ 21st-century marketing techniques. Your M&B Officers should be skilled at establishing brand identity, long-term career planning, and niche marketing. Your M&B Officers will help you increase your professional visibility and credibility within the industry by advising you on how to establish and maintain your brand identity.

Abbey was a 26-year-old therapist specializing in gang-related interventions involving teenage girls. She had a special ability in engaging young women and achieving therapeutic progress in a surprisingly short amount of time. Abbey worked for a nonprofit organization with the mission of helping at-risk female teens, with a focus on preventing teen pregnancy. She ran a girls' therapy group and discovered a common thread among several of her clients: gang involvement. In order to address this contributing factor, Abbey created a special group and a therapeutic protocol that quickly gained traction and proved extremely effective. After she had successfully staged multiple interventions with high-risk teenage female gang members, the word spread, and Abbey received many referrals. She began to devote more of her time to gang interventions.

Because gang issues were not central to the organization's mission, management became concerned with the amount of time Abbey spent on an issue they considered to be her "personal pursuit."

Abbey reached out to Justin, one of her M&B Officers, a well-respected program director. He helped her to assess her current situation, explore her options, and discover where her skills and passions lay. Abbey shared her interest in becoming an expert with female gang interventions. The meeting with Justin helped her to realize that she was undersupported by her supervisor and the administration since her interest was outside the organization's mission. Justin also noted that she had a very limited professional network. Together, they determined that Abbey was very dedicated to the organization and was not interested in making a job move at that time. With Justin's encouragement, plus a few connections from his vast contacts list, Abbey was able to leave the meeting with a plan. Her to-do list included:

- Plan meetings with two directors for Cure Violence programs that target teenage girls.
- Explore LinkedIn groups that focus on leadership development for teens.
- Follow up on an invitation to the Girls Clubs of America's annual conference, where the conference theme was "Gang Intervention." (She had never attended this event in prior years.)

Although Abbey felt supported and rejuvenated after her meeting with her M&B Officer, she realized that she was professionally isolated and had lots of work to do to expand her brand and connections outside of her immediate job. Justin's most important gift to Abbey was helping her to realize that her vision did not have to be limited by her organization's current mission. She might be able to influence her organization by sharing her enhanced wisdom and connections while building her professional brand both inside and outside of her organization.

WORKSHEET: POSSIBLE MARKETING & BRANDING OFFICERS
FOR MY PERSONAL BOARD

Name

Relationship

_____   _____

_____   _____

_____   _____

_____   _____

_____   _____

DIVERSITY & EQUITY OFFICERS

Nobody sees anyone as just an individual; it is human nature for us to classify others in a group. We categorize others based on race, gender, values, or beliefs, contributing to environments that support stereotyping for organization members who are considered outside of the norm (Mannix & Neale, 2005). When this mental grouping conforms to stereotypes about some aspect of the person's identity, such as race, gender, or sexual orientation, it contributes to prejudice and unintentional bias that become part of an organization's culture.

Prejudices based on stereotypes are rarely expressed overtly. They are communicated subtly in the form of **micro-messages**. These are gestures, facial expressions, tones of voice, word choices, eye contact, and interactive nuances that can be either debilitating or empowering to employees and to the power of their leadership. Understanding micro-messages will improve leadership skills (Young, 2003). Receiving these micro-messages can leave an individual feeling slighted or hurt, often confused about whether he or she is being "too sensitive," and can undermine an individual's confidence.

For example, Diana and her colleague Eduardo enter a conference room together for a meeting to discuss progress on a project on which they share responsibility. As they enter, Alex, the senior manager holding the meeting, stands, looks past Diana, and greets Eduardo warmly and welcomes him to the meeting. They exchange friendly banter about a recent football game as everybody takes a seat. Then Alex opens the meeting by saying, "Ed, why don't you get us started with an update on what you've been doing?" Eduardo begins the presentation and nods to Diana, who joins in as they had planned for their shared presentation.

Diana feels good about her presentation but worries that her contributions are not valued. She has a good, although not close, relationship with Alex and would not think he ignored her intentionally. Nonetheless, his behavior did give her the impression that he thinks of Eduardo as the lead on the project, with her as an assistant or helper. Diana is counting on the success of this project to put her in the spotlight for consideration for a promotion in the near future and feels that she needs to do something to follow up.

She approaches two of her Diversity & Equity Officers from her VPBOD separately to discuss the situation and decide how best to respond. One mentor is a man about Alex's age with a similar position of authority in another company. He provides his perspective as a middle-aged, white, male manager and offers that Alex may have been so focused on putting Eduardo, a dark-skinned Latino, at ease that Diana's position as the only woman in the room did not register. He notes that the banter about sports is a way men communicate to one another in that "Hey, we're all on the same team" manner, without realizing, of course, that Diana was implicitly excluded from that team. He recommends that Diana not approach Alex directly about this incident but that she be conscious of her own subtle communications, such as saying "We developed this" rather than appropriate use of statements such as "I took the lead on this part, while Eduardo focused on that part." The goal, her mentor notes, is to communicate her leadership while crediting Eduardo for his work.

Diana's other D&E mentor is a woman only a step ahead of her on her career path. This mentor is able to offer insights from a perspective very close to Diana's experience. With this mentor, Diana gets a sympathetic eye roll and is helped to both laugh and fume about the incident—and then figure out the best next steps. Based on her mentor's advice, Diana decides to talk not to Alex but to Eduardo. Combining insights from both mentors, Diana discusses with Eduardo the benefits of both of them changing their language to take opportunities to highlight personal achievement and leadership while also communicating teamwork. She also decides to share her concerns about micro-messages with Eduardo, to learn if he, too, has had similar experiences or concerns and could be an ally in addition to being a team partner.

WORKSHEET: POSSIBLE DIVERSITY & EQUITY OFFICERS
FOR MY PERSONAL BOARD

Name   Relationship

_____   _____

_____   _____

_____   _____

_____   _____

_____   _____

EDUCATION OFFICERS

Continuing education is one key to personal and professional success. You must commit yourself to improving and expanding your knowledge throughout your career. I advise my mentees and coaching clients to pursue educational opportunities every semester for their entire career. Educational pursuits could include an hourlong webinar, a certificate program, a four-session weekend training seminar, or a biweekly peer supervision group. These should be in addition to any staff development training offered by your employer. Always take advantage of any opportunities that your organization offers, even if you are not able to see their usefulness at the moment. Be open to learning new things; you cannot tell where new skills will take your career or what connections you might make to expand your network. Create a pattern of being a lifelong learner. Add Internet training to your pool of educational options; Skype sessions, blogs, and online specialty groups allow easy access and are often free.

Education Officers can guide your Personal Education Plan (PEP) and advise you on educational pursuits. In order to begin assessing your educational needs, you should reflect on your current position and your ultimate goals. Ask yourself: "What do I need to learn in order to be more proficient at my current job? Do I need an additional degree in order to be better situated during the next phase of my career?" If you want to pursue a leadership role in your organization, you may need to take a leadership course. If you are in private practice, you need to take courses to help you learn how to better manage your business and in order to learn such skills as determining the fees for clients, consulting, and speaking engagements, along with the administrative responsibilities of your office. If you desire a more high-profile role at a nonprofit, attend a seminar on corporate communications. This is the type of guidance your Education Officers will provide to enhance your professional development. Continuing to pursue education will improve your chances of reaching your most lofty professional aspirations. In addition, educational settings are great places to seek out new board members who will help you sharpen your vision and clarify your goals for your professional future.

Your Education Officers will have ideas to supplement your credentials with a higher degree or improve your résumé with additional skills. Your Education Officers are likely people who themselves have many certifications or personal experience with continuing education. You may consult various Education Officers at any given time, depending on the situation. One thing your Education Officers will have in common is a passion for learning and an expertise in pursuing education, especially for the purpose of improving professional know-how and proficiency.

> In today's knowledge-based economy, what you earn depends on what you learn.
>
> US President Bill Clinton

WORKSHEET: POSSIBLE EDUCATION OFFICERS
FOR MY PERSONAL BOARD

Name   Relationship

_____   _____

_____   _____

_____   _____

_____   _____

_____   _____

HEALTH & WELLNESS OFFICERS

It is a given that you need to stay healthy in order to achieve career success. Health & Wellness Officers will help you achieve a healthy balance between your time at work and your time at home. Remember, working 24 hours a day is not a sign of dedication; it is a signal that you have no personal life. It is often a warning sign to professional colleagues that you are challenged in finding balance. Your Heath & Wellness Officers can guide your Personal Wellness Plan (PWP), a document that details your health goals for the future.

Create both physical and mental health plans for your total overall well-being. If you are not physically healthy, it is impossible to be in good form at work. Thriving on the job requires that you maintain physical, mental, and spiritual fitness. A high-stress job or a challenging junction of your career may take a substantial toll on your physical and mental health. If you find yourself unable to cope, you may consider seeking therapy. Also note that physical activity refreshes the mind, body, and spirit.

For example, Dr. Romano, 44, had a very busy psychiatry practice and maintained his PWP by following strict rules about how he managed his time. Dr. Romano had been diagnosed with high blood pressure because of his highly stressful job, long hours, and lack of downtime. Because his father had died of a heart attack at the young age of 45, Dr. Romano was extremely concerned about his diagnosis and decided to make some major changes to his professional routine to improve his health and reduce his chances of suffering a fate similar to his father's. He implemented changes such as ending his workweek on Thursday promptly at 5:00 p.m. and didn't resume work until Monday morning. He would often treat himself to a massage as a ritual to end his workweek. Over the weekend, he monitored his work e-mail and voicemail, but did not answer his phone past 9:00 p.m. except for emergencies—no exceptions. He began taking guitar lessons and joined his friends on hiking trips. He also took a lunch hour every day. Although he might not actually go out to eat, he always set aside an hour during the day to meditate, read, go for a walk, or talk with a friend. In this way, this very busy psychiatrist was able to maintain strict boundaries between his work and personal time.

WORKSHEET: POSSIBLE HEALTH & WELLNESS EXPERTS
FOR MY PERSONAL BOARD

Name   Relationship

_____   _____

_____   _____

_____   _____

_____   _____

_____   _____

MEMBERS-AT-LARGE

A potential mentor who is not a specialist in any particular field but is a generalist with a broad array of knowledge about many different subjects is categorized as a member-at-large of your Personal Board. Members-at-large do not have to be classified under any of the specific offices above. For example, you may have just heard a rumor about downsizing at your organization. This could mean that you will lose your position. It could mean that you are going to get a severance package. It could also mean that you will be assigned more responsibilities, because there will be more work for fewer employees. You may need to consult your Personal Board to figure out what you would do next.

Brainstorming about potential options if you lost your position is a good task for an ad hoc committee. Consult individually with selected board members with various specializations, and then consider their opinions in order to figure out how to get from point A to point B. At this stage, consulting an expert exclusively is counterproductive, because an expert's perspective may be too narrow and therefore misleading. The goal of an ad hoc committee is to garner a broad selection of board members' opinions in order to broaden options and potentially expand your network and the number of connections available to you.

You may also classify potential mentors as members-at-large until you get to know specifically what they have to offer you in terms of knowledge, expertise, and contacts. You need to compile a list, because you need to be clear about each mentor's expertise. The ultimate objective is to assign each board member a specific role on your Virtual Board and mine his or resources and connections. Until you get to know each board member, you could see your relationship as being in a holding pattern. Do not be discouraged if it takes some time to get on solid ground with a mentor. Building meaningful relationships requires time and patience.

WORKSHEET: POSSIBLE MEMBERS-AT-LARGE
FOR MY PERSONAL BOARD

Name   Relationship

_____   _____

_____   _____

_____   _____

_____   _____

_____   _____

_____   _____

_____   _____

_____   _____

_____   _____

_____   _____

_____   _____

_____   _____

_____   _____

FAMOUS MENTORING PAIRS: BUSINESS AND CORPORATE

Mentor	Mentee
J. Paul Austin, former chairman of Coca-Cola	Jack Welch, CEO of General Electric
Warren Buffett, American investor	Donald Graham, publisher of the *Washington Post*
Andrew Carnegie, founder of US Steel	Charles Schwab, founder of Charles Schwab Corporation
W. Edmund Clark, CEO of Canada's TD Bank Group	Colleen Johnston, CEO of Canada's TD Bank Group
Barry Diller, creator of Fox Broadcasting Company	Michael Eisner, CEO of Disney
Millard S. Drexler, CEO of J. Crew	Jenna Lyons, J. Crew designer
Sir Freddie Laker, CEO of Laker Airways	Sir Richard Branson, founder of Virgin Group
Robert McNamara, former US secretary of defense	Lee Iacocca, former president and CEO of Chrysler
Jim Pattison, CEO of the Jim Pattison Group	Nick Geer, former president and CEO of Insurance Corporation of British Columbia
Ayn Rand, American novelist	Alan Greenspan, former chairman of the Federal Reserve Bank
Steve Ross, former CEO of Time Warner	Dick Parsons, chairman and CEO of Time Warner
Sidney Weinberg, former CEO of Goldman Sachs	Henry Ford, founder and CEO of Ford Motor Company
John Rowe Workman, former Brown University classics professor	Ted Turner, founder of CNN

PROFILES IN MENTORSHIP: ANNE MULCAHY AND URSULA BURNS

Interesting facts about mentoring pair Anne Mulcahy and Ursula Burns:

- When Mulcahy (figure 4.1) handed stewardship of Xerox over to Burns in 2009, it represented the first-ever woman-to-woman transfer of the CEO role in the Fortune 500.
- Burns (figure 4.2) is the first black female to lead a Fortune 500 company in the role of CEO.

FIGURE 4.1 Mentor: Anne Mulcahy, CEO and chairwoman of Xerox, 2001–2009.

FIGURE 4.2 Mentee: Ursula Burns, CEO of Xerox, 2009–present.

Anne Mulcahy

Mulcahy was told by her mentor, "When everything gets really complicated and you feel overwhelmed, you gotta do three things: first, get the cow out of the ditch; second, find out how the cow got into the ditch; and third, make sure you do whatever it takes so the cow doesn't go in the ditch again."

Ursula Burns

"Where you are is not who you are," was Burns's mother's most cherished advice. "Impatience is a virtue," Burns said. "If you settle in and do only what previous leaders did, you'll be 'run over by change.' You have to set an aspirational path and be impatient to achieve it."

And "You have to first love it and then you'll be good at it. Relax and go after something that you love."

KNOWLEDGE NUGGETS

- The most important conceptual—and structural—component of the Virtual Personal Board of Directors is the board member.
- The VPBOD does not make decisions by committee—the choices are all up to you.
- The mentoring VPBOD functions like a board of advisors: the CEO takes all opinions into consideration and synthesizes them and then makes his or her own decision.
- The VPBOD is made up of 12 board positions, or offices, plus members-at-large:
  - Chief Executive Officer
  - Chairperson of the Board
  - Chief Technical Officer
  - Chief Financial Officer
  - Professional Guru
  - Chief Political Analyst
  - Chief Legal Advisor
  - Ethics & Morals Officer
  - Marketing & Branding Officer
  - Diversity & Equity Officer
  - Education Officer
  - Health & Wellness Expert
  - Members-at-Large
- Each office of your VPBOD will be represented by more than one mentor, organized into a first string, a second string, a third string, and so on, to ensure that a mentor from each office is always available for consultation and also to make available a range of opinions in each board area.

CHAPTER 5

GOAL SETTING FOR YOUR PERSONAL BOARD

Twenty years from now you will be more disappointed by the things that you didn't do than by the ones you did do.

Mark Twain

EMBRACE YOUR PASSION, FIND YOUR MOTIVATION

The Virtual Personal Board of Directors is designed to help you find and embrace your passion in your career, and the first, and most important, step is to establish clear goals. In this chapter, aside from clarifying your vision of your future, we will also:

- Brainstorm the specific types of mentors who can guide and support you in achieving these goals.
- Create a potential board member list, drawing upon people whom you admire and emulate among your friends, family, colleagues, and even celebrities as invisible mentors.
- Assess your potential board member list, correlating each mentor with a specific goal. Identify goals that are not assigned a board member.
- Mine your network to connect with members whose experience and expertise are suited to assist you in the pursuit of those specific objectives.

Once you identify your list of potential board members, it is time to start setting up meetings. Some possible mentors will be eliminated immediately, before you even meet, simply because they are unavailable or inaccessible. Others will be eliminated after your first meeting because of a lack of synergy between the two of you. Remember, you are not formally inviting these people to serve on your board. The VPBOD is a purely mental construct; board members need not be aware of their role in order to provide effective mentoring. Once relationships are well established, your primary mentors may become conscious of their role on your Personal Board. However, the mentor-mentee arrangement is fluid and always fluctuating. You need not forge an explicit agreement with the mentors of your Personal Board, which reduces the pressure of such a relationship to both mentor and mentee. A how-to guide on meeting with potential mentors follows in Chapter 6.

With that overall process in mind, let's get started on your first step to building a VPBOD: formulating, analyzing, and specifying concrete professional goals. Remember, you are the founder, president, and CEO of your Virtual Personal Board. What you do—and what you choose not to do—is *all* up to you.

WHAT ARE YOUR CAREER GOALS?

> People with clear, written goals accomplish far more in a shorter period of time than people without them could ever imagine.
>
> Brian Tracy

In order to create an effective and useful Personal Board, you must have a clear idea of your overall professional direction. If you don't know where you are going, you cannot figure out the right people you need to help you get there. Although much of the VPBOD methodology consists of externally focused tasks, such as reaching out to colleagues and networking for contacts, the underlying foundation of your Personal Board relies on intimate knowledge of your own aspirations and ambitions. Part of the role of a mentor is to help clarify and expand your goals. Once you know your goals, you can determine the corresponding area of the board you need to leverage to help you achieve them. Then you may identify, meet with, and, it's hoped, integrate the specific mentors onto your board who can help you identify immediate, intermediary, and ultimately long-term professional objectives.

Meeting with board members can help with formulating your goals, because they often ask the question that you may not have thought about before: What do you really want? What do you enjoy? What is your passion? Where do you see yourself in six months? One year? You should continually analyze and reevaluate your career goals and, at the very least, do a formal assessment every year to adjust to your changing knowledge and the needs of your profession. Because of the ever-changing nature of the professional climate, flexibility is key. Don't lock yourself into firm long-term goals. Remaining flexible and open to unanticipated opportunities allows you to tweak your career to respond to your passion and to changes in the professional landscape. The most important question to ask yourself is: "What would I do if I were not afraid of failing?"

The direction your internal reflection takes depends on where you are career-wise. If you are employed, decide if you are happy in your current position first. Then identify the parts of your job that you are good at, that you enjoy, and that inspire passion. Everyone—employed or not—should consider his or her ideal job if money were not an object. If you are unemployed and searching for a job, building your Personal Board is of the utmost importance. You should consider drafting to your board the most helpful colleagues to consult in your job search and maintain these relationships after you land a position. If you are still in school, do not think it is too early to start building your VPBOD; this is an ideal time to explore every aspect of your chosen path. Ask for meetings with professors and instructors, career counselors, guest lecturers, and peers you meet either in classes or during extracurricular activities, and begin building your board early.

Ultimately, self-reflection enables you to identify your ideal job's qualities. By determining your passions and gaining clarity about your own personality, you are better able to ascertain your desired job's attributes and craft your professional future. There are many ways to proactively determine the features of your ideal job. One way to gain firsthand experience—including the nitty-gritty details that are left out of textbooks—is to shadow a mentor who has the job you are pursuing. You can also volunteer for short-term assignments at organizations you might want to work for.

You should make a list outlining your dream job's most appealing attributes; for example, working with children, telecommuting, flextime benefits, or working with the public are the types of qualities that could be on your list. If you thoroughly examine your own talents and inclinations alongside the qualities of your intended job, you can avoid making a mistake such as pursuing an MBA even though you can't stand math or going for an MD when the sight of blood makes you woozy.

WORKSHEET: SELF-EXPLORATION QUESTIONNAIRE

1. Five activities or tasks, such as "public speaking," "fundraising," or "teaching others," that make me happy, either on or off the job.

   a. _____

   b. _____

   c. _____

   d. _____

   e. _____

2. What type(s) of job(s) would I pursue if money were not an object?

   _____

   _____

3. What are five personality traits that I consider unique about myself?

   a. _____

   b. _____

   c. _____

   d. _____

   e. _____

4. What activities make me feel good when I do them?

   _____

5. According to my colleagues, which talents and abilities of mine make me stand out?

   _____

6. With what types of colleagues do I most enjoy collaborating?

   _____

7. Where do I see myself in one year?

   _____

8. Where do I see myself in three years?

_____

9. Is my current career my true calling or just a vocation in life?

_____

10. Are there things I have always wanted to do that I haven't done yet? What are they?

_____

11. Are there things I have always wanted to learn that I have not yet explored? What are they?

_____

12. What types of opportunities would I be interested in?

_____

DEFINE AND REFINE YOUR CAREER GOALS WITH A PERSONAL BOARD

No one lives long enough to learn everything they need to learn starting from scratch. To be successful, we absolutely, positively have to find people who have already paid the price to learn the things that we need to learn to achieve our goals.

Brian Tracy

Well-considered goal setting is both a precondition for setting up an effective Personal Board and a consequence of maintaining one. In order to structure and staff your board in a way appropriate for your unique aspirations, position, and personality, you must delve deeply to establish who you are, what you want, and what you need. Once you have a solid foundation in this area, you are ready to craft your board. The first step is identifying a variety of potential mentors and then scheduling meetings with them. Preparation for these initial meetings is crucial: make a list of questions to ask, and reflect on the specific qualities that drew you to these mentors in the first place.

Remember, at board member meetings, you are not looking for references, referrals, or a job. Although any of these outcomes may arise from the meeting, your goal is to understand their interests and passions and search out common interests and goals. First, ascertain your potential board member's position, experience, and areas of expertise. Second, evaluate this person on a personal level in order to determine compatibility. After meetings, document everything you learned. You will later use this information to vet your goals list, assign mentors to positions on your board, and strategize how best to leverage mentoring resources.

Aside from learning new information, the third objective of these initial meetings is to seek your potential mentor's feedback in terms of his or her evaluation of your personal and professional qualities. Solicit each potential mentor's opinion about what it takes to succeed in his or her profession, along with anecdotes about how his or her colleagues have succeeded in the position. Over the course of your queries, you can learn about aspects of the profession that could be exactly suited to your strengths, talents, and interests that you did not know previously. On the other hand, your mentor-to-be may inform you of factors related to his or her field that are a complete turnoff. Whatever the case, you are gleaning invaluable facts that are crucial to your future decision-making process.

The fourth objective of conducting these meetings is to mine your potential mentor for specialized resources, such as connections to organizations or colleagues who may be of further assistance, in addition to leads to opportunities in and outside your field. You should leave each of these meetings armed with a fresh perspective, deeper insight into your professional goals, and a better sense of what position, profession, or field you want—or do not want—to pursue.

What about when you don't know your goals? In this case, you should conduct as many meetings with as many diverse professionals as you can brainstorm. If you are unsure of the field or profession you want to consider, then meet with inspirational individuals from any field that happens to get you curious. Research positions that appeal to you *before* meeting with potential board members; in doing so, you will eliminate certain options and gain more interest in others. Researching beforehand will also enable you to be prepared with pertinent questions to ask potential mentors-to-be during fact-finding meetings. Do not limit yourself, and keep an open mind.

WORKSHEET: MY TOP 10 CAREER GOALS

List the top 10 goals you want to accomplish in your career. Enumerate them one by one, and then organize them in order of priority by annotating each line item in the second column with a rating on a scale from 1 to 5, 1 for "not that important" and 5 for "top priority." We will use these ratings in other worksheets in the following chapters. Some examples:

Goal	Rating
I would like to become a manager.	4
I would like to start my own private practice.	3
I want to become the president of NASW.	5
I want to teach at a school of social work.	5
_____	_____
_____	_____
_____	_____
_____	_____
_____	_____
_____	_____
_____	_____
_____	_____
_____	_____
_____	_____

WORKSHEET: FEATURES OF MY IDEAL JOB

List the qualities you can envision as features of your dream job. Think about organizational culture. Would you prefer a formal hierarchy or a casual, creative environment? Enumerate the features one by one, and then organize them in order of priority by annotating each with a rating on a scale from 1 to 5; 1 for "not that important" and 5 for "deal maker." We will use these ratings in other worksheets in the following chapters. Some examples:

Job Quality or Feature	Rating
I would like a creative work environment.	4
I would like to work with children under 5.	5
I would like to travel at least 50% of the time.	3
_____	_____
_____	_____
_____	_____
_____	_____
_____	_____

WORKSHEET: POTENTIAL BOARD MEMBER BRAINSTORM

On this worksheet, you will construct a master list of potential mentors, organized by board position. Review the list of individuals you brainstormed under each board position in chapter 4, and enter their names in the corresponding categories. Strive to identify at least four candidates for each position. Remember, you can list invisible mentors, too. Board building is a gradual process. Time, patience, and persistence are key to developing a masterful Personal Board. Some examples are given below.

Board Position	Candidate and Title	Notes
Chairperson of the Board	*John Smith, director of HR*	*Can give advice on vetting new hires*
	Mary Jones, IT manager	*Can help me select proper project management software*
Chief Technical Officers		
Chief Financial Officers		

Professional Gurus		
Chief Political Analysts		
Legal Advisors		
Ethics & Morals Officers		
Marketing & Branding Officers		

Diversity & Equity Officers		
Education Officers		
Health & Wellness Officers		
Members-at-Large		

DOCUMENTING BOARD MEMBER MEETINGS

You need to do work both *before* and *after* all meetings with potential and current board members. You will notate each mentor meeting in a journal and make notes about important information: their feedback, the answers to your questions, their advice on your next steps, the names and contact information of references and referrals, and any special knowledge or information you gleaned during the meeting. Be sure to make notes on your own or your mentor's follow-up tasks. In the following chapters, we will discuss the Rules of Engagement for board member interactions in more depth.

WORKSHEET: MENTOR MEETING JOURNAL

Mentor Name, Title, Company	Feedback About Me	Meeting Takeaway	Next Steps to Follow Up
Mary Jones, VP of marketing at ABC Corp, Inc.	Positive: I am thorough and detail-oriented. Needs improvement: I don't assert myself; I am not proactive about pursuing training opportunities.	I need to assert myself with coworkers.	Register for a training course with HR. Remind Mary to do an eIntroduction to Harold Jones if her e-mail is not received by Friday.

ORGANIZING YOUR PERSONAL BOARD

Congratulations! You are now well on the way to commencing the board-building process. Remember, your Virtual Personal Board will never be "finished" or "complete." The VPBOD is built on a fluid structure that you may continually adapt to your professional needs at any point in time.

Once you fill top-level slots, you will gradually build your Personal Board roster's second-string, third-string, and subsequent positions. Some board offices will require a larger roster of mentors than other offices, depending on your specific profession and the position you currently hold. For example, if you are a malpractice attorney, you may not require multiple Legal Advisors but instead will staff your Professional Guru roster with many doctors, nurses, and other medical professionals. Board development is not a linear process. The goal is to build each board office until you have enough members to meet your current needs and continue adding special people for possible future needs.

Once the self-reflection process is complete and you have determined your goals and aspirations, it is time to focus on external tasks such as networking with colleagues and adding mentors to all areas of your board. You are now thinking, communicating, and acting like the CEO of your Virtual Personal Board. Now you must become an expert in VPBOD structure so that you can create your own unique Personal Board that reflects your values and personality and is squarely targeted on your future professional aspirations. In chapter 6, we will begin building your VPBOD.

WORKSHEET: MENTOR CONTACT DIRECTORY

Keep your entire roster of all potential, current, and past board members, organized in a contact directory such as the one below. Reflect on each board prospect, and annotate with title, position, and company; outstanding qualities; who introduced you or how you met; and contact information. The following table may serve as a template for a custom directory that you can create in Excel or Word, implement in Outlook or another contact management application, or use online with Gmail or other online contact apps. You can also use the complimentary app that corresponds to the VPBOD system online www.VirtualPersonalBoard. com, which provides an array of mentor management tools, including a contact directory.

Name	Title, Company	Outstanding Qualities	Contact Information	Referred By
Mary Jones	VP of marketing at ABC Corp, Inc.	Well versed in cutting-edge digital marketing techniques Woman in a prominent corporate position Teaches a business administration course	mary.jones@ email.com	Met at sales conference, July 2013

YOU'RE READY TO BUILD YOUR
PERSONAL BOARD

Every professional likely has individuals who are functionally serving as board members even if he or she does not formally maintain a VPBOD. When setting out to build your board, the first thing you should do is consider the individuals closest to you who are already performing the role and evaluate if their role as advisor should be virtually formalized into a position on your board. Remember, board members are not aware of their roles on your board; you may get as much guidance out of a board member role model who doesn't even know you exist as you do from a close personal mentor whom you speak to on a weekly basis.

You should not limit yourself when choosing board members. Your Personal Board is a virtual construct, so you may staff it with famous people or industry icons you have never met. If you are drawn to them and their work inspires you, then they have a place on your Personal Board, even if only as role models you can admire and emulate from afar. You don't need to have one-on-one conversations with someone in order for his or her to function as an effective board member. Simply observe and absorb everything possible about the person's life story and professional accomplishments. Read potential mentors' books and articles, voraciously take in any media presentations, and attend their public appearances. Thanks to the Internet, "following" the careers of role models is now easier then ever. Follow their Twitter feeds, "like" them on Facebook, and subscribe to their YouTube channel—it's that simple! Invisible mentoring (which was discussed in detail in chapter 2) is an easy way of having a superstar, however inaccessible, on your Personal Board, without one-on-one, personal interaction.

FAMOUS MENTORING PAIRS: INTERNET AND HIGH-TECH

Mentor	Mentee
Sergey Brin, cofounder of Google	Marissa Mayer, president and CEO of Yahoo
Warren Buffett, American investor	Bill Gates, cofounder of Microsoft
John Chambers, chairman and CEO of Cisco Systems	Donald Listwin, CEO of Sana Security
Larry Ellison, CEO of Oracle	Marc Benioff, founder and CEO of Salesforce.com
Robert Friedland, founder of Ivanhoe Mines	Steve Jobs, cofounder of Apple
Andrew Grove, cofounder of Intel	Steve Jobs, cofounder of Apple
Steve Jobs, cofounder of Apple	Larry Page, cofounder of Google
Steve Jobs, cofounder of Apple	Mark Zuckerberg, founder of Facebook
Anne Mulcahy, chairwoman and CEO of Xerox	Ursula Burns, CEO of Xerox
Robert Noyce, cofounder of Intel	Steve Jobs, cofounder of Apple
Ed Roberts, founder of MITS and inventor of the personal computer	Bill Gates, cofounder of Microsoft
Eric Schmidt, executive chairman of Google	Marissa Mayer, president and CEO of Yahoo

PROFILES IN MENTORSHIP: STEVE JOBS AND THE CHAIN OF MENTORSHIP

> What we have done for ourselves alone dies with us. What we have done for others and the world remains and is immortal.
>
> Albert Pine

One example of how important the "chain of mentorship" is to facilitating the expansion and success of any given industry is the mentoring choices of tech genius Steve Jobs, founder and CEO of Apple Computer (figure 5.1). Jobs's career profoundly changed not only the entire computer industry but also the entire world. We would be living very differently today had Jobs not existed—or succeeded.

FIGURE 5.1 Mentor: Steve Jobs, cofounder of Apple.

Jobs accomplished his professional goals in large part as a result of very wise mentoring choices throughout his career. In his younger years, while still in college, he sought out the mentoring of two influential computing geniuses: Robert Noyce and Andrew Grove, collaborators on the invention of the microchip and cofounders of Intel Corporation. Without the guidance of Noyce and Grove, Jobs may not have embraced his innovative vision for revolutionizing personal computing. Even though Intel was, in the early years, a competitor to Apple, Jobs maintained the relationships and sought the highly valued advice of the "Fathers of Personal Computing" concerning the development of his own hardware products and proprietary operating system—despite the potential obvious risks.

Eventually, Jobs chose to integrate the Intel microchip into his products, marking the point where Apple's dominance of the personal computing market in terms of both hardware and software was uncontested. When Jobs became one of the "old guard" of the computing and high-tech industries, he began to serve as mentor to some of the most influential businessmen of the new millennium. Sergey Brin and Larry Page, cofounders of Google, looked to Jobs for guidance and support in creating and marketing the algorithm that ultimately became the most widely used search engine in the marketplace. Marc Benioff of Salesforce.com (figure 5.2) was also mentored by Jobs, in fact, Benioff was so grateful for Jobs's invaluable advice that he granted Apple the App Store trademark free of charge, something unheard of in today's profit-oriented economy. Mark Zuckerberg of Facebook fame (figure 5.3) also credits the mentorship of Jobs as being central in the success of his social networking company. "We saw eye to eye on kind of what we were trying to do in the world," Zuckerberg said of Jobs in a 2011 interview on *Charlie Rose*, and he also shared that Jobs gave him advice on developing a management team that was "focused on building as high quality and good things as you are."

In fact, multigenerational mentorship pervades the world of high-tech, and the Internet in particular, which makes sense considering that the Web is all about interconnectivity. High-tech is an example of what a positive impact effective mentoring can have. This cyclical, symbiotic, self-sustaining chain of mentorship played a central role in the personal computing and Internet revolution of the turn of the millennium. Jobs served as the conduit channeling the technological innovations of the 20th century into the 21st. This is one of the most important roles of mentorship in society: preserving knowledge across generations and establishing and maintaining continuity within an industry. The illustrious career of Jobs is one of the most dramatic examples of how the institution of mentorship actually was responsible for completely changing every aspect of not only technology but also culture and society. There is not one element of modern life that the work of Jobs does not continue to influence to this day. In a very definite way, Jobs's professional success—and the myriad advancements that came with it—can be attributed to the ages-old institution of mentorship.

STEVE JOBS'S MENTEES REFLECT ON HIS INFLUENCE

Marc Benioff of Salesforce.com on Steve Jobs

FIGURE 5.2 Mentee: Marc Benioff, founder and CEO of Salesforce.com.

"He has probably given me more help and more advice than just about anybody. When I get in trouble, and when I get lost in my own vision, I've been fortunate to go and see him, and he's been able to show me the future a couple times when I got lost in the forest for the trees. One really good example of that happened in 2003. I went down to talk to him and brought a few members of my executive team. He said something really exciting: 'Look, you've got a fantastic enterprise application here, but you've gotta build an ecosystem.' So, to us, we went back and we're, like, 'well, we don't know how to do that.'

"That was like a Zen koan. How do we build an ecosystem? So we designed this whole technology that we called 'App Store' that was the ability to buy these apps and run them in Salesforce. And when we launched it, we called it AppExchange, and you can see it at AppExchange.com. But we liked the App Store name so much that we bought the URL and trademarked it, and then I was in the audience when he announced the App Store, and I went up to him, and I said, 'I have a gift for you. I'm going to give you the trademark and the URL for the help you gave me in 2003.'"

Mark Zuckerberg of Facebook on Steve Jobs
"He's amazing. He was amazing. I had a lot of questions for him. . . .
How to build a team around you, that's focused on building as high-quality and good things as you are. How to keep an organization focused, when I think the tendency for larger companies is to try to fray and go into all these different

FIGURE 5.3 Mentee: Mark Zuckerberg, founder of Facebook.

areas. Yeah, a lot just on the aesthetics and kind of mission orientation of companies. I mean, Apple is a company that is so focused on just building products for their customers and their users. And it's such a deep part of their mission is build these beautiful products for their users. And I think we connected a lot on this level of, OK, Facebook has this mission that's really more than just trying to build a company, which has a market cap or a value. It's like we're trying to do this thing in the world. And I just think we connected on that level.

KNOWLEDGE NUGGETS

- The first, and most important, step to building a Virtual Personal Board of Directors is to establish clear, defined goals of where you want to go in your career in both the long and the short term.
- Self-exploration about your true passions, innate talents, and innermost desires is the fundamental building block toward creating an effective and successful Virtual Personal Board.
- Choose potential mentors who have the specific skills, knowledge, and contacts that will assist you in clarifying and achieving your overall goals.
- Employ organizational and planning tools such as a potential mentor contact journal and your app to maximize the productivity of your Virtual Personal Board.

CHAPTER 6

BUILDING YOUR VIRTUAL BOARD

> Most people can do absolutely awe-inspiring things. Sometimes they just need a little nudge.
>
> Timothy Ferriss

CRAFTING YOUR VIRTUAL PERSONAL BOARD OF DIRECTORS

Putting together your Virtual Personal Board of Directors requires careful planning, conscious effort, and calculated thought. A well-staffed Personal Board does not just happen by accident. Crafting a Personal Board that enhances your ability to make career decisions and improves your professional performance is both a science and an art. The Personal Board is a practice rooted in scientific methodology and characterized by steadfast principles, hereafter referred to as the Rules of Engagement, which one must learn and apply. However, crafting a Personal Board is also an art, requiring an intuitive sense and a creative mindset in order to create a personalized circle of mentors with whom the mentee feels a sense of synergy.

Most important, you need to consider whom to appoint to your board. Choose people strategically based on the unique qualities they bring to the table. Select individuals who can guide you in your chosen career or teach you important principles or information that you do not yet know. Think of the members of your board as a panel of specialists with whom you consult on a case-by-case basis when the need arises, just as CEOs do with their corporate boards. Your mentors should know more than you do about the various areas that make up the offices of the Virtual Personal Board. If a board member is not selected for specialized knowledge, he or she should offer a different point of view or perspective to which you would otherwise not have access.

You also need to know where to look for potential board members. In addition to family and friends, you can also consider prior colleagues, former employers, employees, supervisors, speakers, workshop leaders, teachers, professors, students, and connections from social media such as Facebook, Twitter, and LinkedIn. You may encounter a potential board member in any of these places, so always keep your eyes open.

In order to build a well-functioning board, it is important to become familiar with the Rules of Engagement and stick to them when forging relationships with potential mentors. Remember, fostering and maintaining a balanced mix of different mentor types is crucial to creating a well-rounded board. While all of your board members should be individuals you hold in high regard, some of them should be people who know you well, such as friends, family, and associates, and not only professional colleagues or peers. A contingent of mentors who genuinely care about you will be invested emotionally in your professional success and will therefore go the extra mile as your champions. However, it is equally important to staff your board with mentors who are *not* emotionally tied to the results of your decisions. In addition, it is essential that your board feature diversity in terms of gender, race, career stage, age, and cultural and political perspectives.

Fresh thinkers connected with younger generations are also an absolute must for a well-balanced Personal Board. For seasoned and mid-career professionals, incorporating younger board members enable you to forge connections you otherwise would not have. The concept of more mature professionals being mentored by younger people is called reverse mentorship and will be discussed in more detail. The higher up you move in your career, especially once you achieve an executive role, the more out of touch you can become with the rank-and-file and fresh young thinkers in your profession. This contributes to the stagnation of your thinking and your career. Likewise, corporate boards can become irrelevant if the board members only talk among themselves and do not benefit from the innovative and unique perspectives of younger, more forward-thinking people.

Finding the right board members is crucial and requires time, tenacity, and the willingness to risk rejection. Keep in mind that the most qualified potential board members are likely to be busy individuals. Therefore, when it comes to making a connection with a board member, have patience. Board building is a continual process that evolves over many years. It is a process that is never really complete. You will constantly restructure and develop your Personal Board. You will continuously tweak the membership by shifting board members' roles, adding new members, and phasing out current members.

DETERMINE WHOM YOU NEED FOR YOUR PERSONAL BOARD

Surround yourself with the dreamers and the doers, the believers and thinkers, but most of all, surround yourself with those who see greatness within you, even when you don't see it yourself.

Edmund Lee

To determine potential members to appoint to your Virtual Personal Board, think about people whose careers and lives you have found exciting and inspiring. You won't find these special, unique individuals easily all in one place. To quote Ross Perot (figure 6.1), "Eagles

FIGURE 6.1 Ross Perot, American businessman.

don't flock; you have to find them one at a time." The same holds true for board members. Your board should be made up of distinct and exceptional individuals. The way you find these leaders is one at a time, in diverse settings, and through varying methods. In addition to the traditional source pools for mentors, be on the lookout for potential board members in atypical settings such as at the health club, at a spa, on vacation, and on the golf course.

As you build your professional posse, remember that every board member should not only be distinctive and exceptional but should also be the best possible match for *you* specifically. Take your time cultivating relationships in order to find ideal board members who can fulfill the needs of helping you achieve your particular professional goals. Focus on the special people with whom you have a distinct connection and with whom you feel synergy.

The major reason for your VPBOD is to help you to become your **best self**, in both a professional and an individual sense. Keep in mind that each board member relationship requires time and nurturing. Throughout the life of your career, you will constantly seek new members whose work and vision matches your own evolving professional focus. Remember, board cultivation is a continual process that sometimes yields immediate results but is more often a long-term proposition. Cultivating a well-rounded board must be seen as an extremely prudent investment in your professional and personal future, not a race to the finish line.

> The greatest good you can do for another is not just to share your riches but to reveal to him his own.
>
> Benjamin Disraeli

Just as you need fresh young thinkers on your board, it is also important to include experienced seasoned professionals from previous generations. With baby boomers beginning to retire, many are looking back at their previous and idealistic goals of changing the world. These individuals are prime candidates for board membership, because many still have goals, missions, and legacies to fulfill. Therefore, connecting with mentors from this generation can represent a win-win for both mentor and protégé. Acting as a board member is an extremely rewarding experience, especially later in one's career, when many more mature professionals are seeking avenues for remaining connected to their field and ways to "pay it forward" by helping others.

Choose mentors from diverse professions in order to move "outside the box" of your field. The more diverse your board, the better it will meet your needs. Each board member should be chosen strategically for their distinctive qualities; focus on board members' unique qualities and specific areas of expertise. Remember, your board will be made up of experts whose primary role is to enhance your life by helping you to become your best self. Using the VPBOD system is akin to having your own personal knowledge base customized to your specific professional needs. Board members gain pleasure from witnessing your growth and seeing their connections pay off for you.

> Unless we think of others and do something for them, we miss one of the greatest sources of happiness.
>
> Ray Lyman Wilbur

SOURCE POOLS FOR POTENTIAL BOARD MEMBERS

You will encounter potential board members at the most diverse places, such as the office break room, workshops, networking events, and social media. You should be on the lookout for potential additions to your VPBOD everywhere you go, including all social interactions. The following, however, are the most likely places where you will find an individual you would like to add to your Personal Board:

- Professional conferences.
- National membership organization of your profession.
- On the job or at the workplace.
- National conventions.
- Annual meetings.
- College, university, or continuing education classes.
- Alumni functions such as reunions.
- Civic and charity events.
- Social or family gatherings.
- Online groups and social media sites such as Facebook and LinkedIn.

- Online webinars, chat rooms, and message boards.
- After-work social events (such as your office holiday party).

Anybody with whom you feel a particular connection is a potential member of your board. When you meet someone special, take his or her business card and put it in your contacts database. Creating a VPBOD electronic journal is a good way to keep track of potential board members. You can also use the complementary app that corresponds to the VPBOD system online at www.VirtualPersonalBoard.com, which provides an array of mentor management tools and a contact directory.

PROSPECTING FOR BOARD MEMBERS

> Your personal success is tied to your ability to build a network of people who you can look to for help and advice.
>
> Jerry Bruckner

There is no special way, place, or technique for meeting prospective mentors. Be on the lookout at all times—in the office, on a plane, or at a conference. You never can tell where a perfectly suited board member will be found. Be clear about the kinds of things that are missing in your board. You are looking for synergy with a specific person. Be open to new ideas and expanding beyond your regular routine. Joining a new online group or attending the annual conference of an allied profession are things that will expand your pool of board candidates.

IDENTIFY POTENTIAL BOARD MEMBERS WHOM YOU KNOW

Think about the people in your life who have inspired you, whom you admire, and with whom you enjoy a sense of camaraderie. This could include immediate or distant family members, neighbors, schoolmates, or friends from your past or present. Also reflect on individuals who have expressed an interest in your success and have been curious about your professional pursuits. Most likely, you have been drawn to each other because you are naturally compatible. This natural synergy is one of the most valuable qualities in a mentor. Approaching family members or other acquaintances to serve on your board is not as intimidating or daunting as seeking the mentorship of a stranger or an unfamiliar professional, so it is a good place to start.

If you don't have relationships in your field, think about peers, colleagues, office staff, neighbors, past classmates, teachers, fraternity or sorority members, and congregants from your house of worship. Join your school alumni organization, a professional association, or civic groups (condo association, PTA, political group, etc.).

IDENTIFY COLLEAGUES FROM YOUR OWN FIELD

Start with professionals you already know in your own field. Make a list of those who have impressed you or whom you look up to. You can include people in your current organization and in previous places of employment. You should also consider individuals who may be part of a competing organization. Just because you don't work at the same place, that does not mean this person cannot be a resource for you. Consider peers and colleagues who are younger or newer to the profession than you are. You never know what skills or connections a new member might bring regardless of his or her station in life.

IDENTIFY IMPRESSIVE PROFESSIONALS FROM OUTSIDE YOUR FIELD

Remember, you want your Personal Board to be wide-ranging and diverse. Include professionals from outside your particular field. Think of accessible individuals you already know who inspire you. If you do not know them personally, connect with them through networking.

IDENTIFY POTENTIAL BOARD MEMBERS FROM YOUR PAST AND RECONNECT

There may be people with whom you worked or had a previous relationship who made an impression on you. You can reconnect with people from your past by appointing them to your Personal Board. This can include past schoolmates, professors, former neighbors, or family friends.

IDENTIFY INACCESSIBLE ROLE MODELS TO SERVE AS INVISIBLE MENTORS

Celebrities or superstars in your field may not be accessible to serve personally on your board. However, by using the modality of invisible mentoring, you can benefit from their careers. Invisible mentors serve as role models for your own professional development.

THE NEXT STEP: BEGIN MEETING WITH BOARD MEMBERS

Once you identify your goals and needs and prospect for and identify potential board members, the next step in building your VPBOD is to schedule meetings. Your aim is to have dozens of meetings with many different people when you commence the board-building process. The goal is to expand your network of people to help you gain more knowledge about the field. You are looking for new connections and opportunities to expand your knowledge about your profession and allied fields.

Even if there is no synergy in a meeting with someone, he or she might still be able to help you make other connections that will prove to be valuable. Some of your best referrals may originate with people you only meet once, who could potentially connect you with someone with whom you establish a lifelong relationship.

Choose some individuals from outside your profession. The more diverse your board is, the better it can meet your needs. Remember to keep your needs and their unique qualities in mind.

TOPICS TO REFLECT ON BEFORE MEETING WITH A POTENTIAL BOARD MEMBER

Regarding one's career: Always be prepared, no shortcuts—hard work is the only alternative that really works.

Kiana Tom

- What is your interest in this person? What makes him or her special?
- Come up with questions after you have done research but don't just ask questions. Share your thoughts, opinions, and feelings so they can get to know you.
- Listen more than you talk. You want to find out how this person will be able to help you.
- Keep in mind that a mentor's value lies not only in what he or she can personally do for you but also in his or her influence and ability to connect you to others through networking.
- Consider the specific nature of assistance you need in your career, now or in the future.

Do not be discouraged if it is difficult to get a meeting with a potential mentor on your first invitation. You may have to work hard to schedule a meeting with the "eagles" and the gurus. They might cancel at the last minute, or you may have to wait three months for an available appointment. But keep at it! The reward is well worth the wait. In addition, your tenacity will impress the person even before you meet.

When you don't know what your goals are, you meet with interesting people and talk to them about what they are doing. The goal is to learn what you don't know and to discover the things you didn't realize that you didn't know. It would be helpful if he or she is doing things that are interesting to you. Reflecting on these conversations helps you to gain a deeper understanding of the role and the profession so you can make an informed decision about your career. Did speaking to this person bore you or excite you? Remember, it takes times, tenacity, and the willingness to risk rejection to find the appropriate board members for *you*.

HOW TO PREPARE FOR BOARD MEMBER MEETINGS

One important task is to work on your vision beforehand so that you can sharpen it with each encounter. The other part is to be open to listening and mining for knowledge nuggets that you were not aware of, aspects of the profession, and intricate areas that may be of interest to you.

You need to do work *before* and *after* you meet with a board member, whether he or she is currently serving or is merely a potential mentor. This checklist will help you prepare for both preliminary board member meetings and meetings with references, mentors, and anyone you want to mine for knowledge and information. Set aside time before each meeting to review this checklist and formulate your meeting agenda to avoid wasting your *or* your mentor's time.

You should to do plenty of listening so you can leave the meeting enriched and full of new information. Although you should also ask questions, focus on listening and learning. Look for opportunities to offer something of value to your board member in exchange for the time and effort he or she spends advising and guiding you as a member of your board. The goal is not to give something to the mentor at the meeting but more to come to understand how you might be able to offer something. It is not payment in the traditional sense, where there is an immediate exchange for services rendered. The relationship is a two-way street; you want to think of things you can add that might be of interest to the mentor. Look for things you have in common or things you might bring to the table, such as your network of connections, your passion for technology, or your knowledge about social media.

If you don't have anything before the meeting, keep an ear out for what you can bring to the relationship. You have more to offer than you imagine.

The best mentor-mentee relationships are ones that are symbiotic; in other words, each party does something for the other. Creative mentorship is about give and take. Even if the person isn't perfect for your board, keep him or her in the fold, because you may be able to refer that person to a colleague's board. Keep in mind that your goal is to build a network and expand your influence, to become a connector, so that all you need can be found in your network and keep an open mind about all your mentors—current, past, or potential. If you approach relationships with a closed mind, you will not be able to connect with people and mine the gems that they can offer to your network. In other words, without the connection, they will not offer you access to their wisdom, resources, or influence.

Before meeting with mentor candidates:

- Make sure to research them.
- Never ask them things about themselves or their business that can be found out beforehand.

- Work on your professional vision before each visit, and have a goal of sharpening it with each encounter. The goal is to find out how this person can help you define and reach your goals.
- Limit your goals with each board member to two or three.
- Cast a wide net.
- You still need to meet with people even when you don't have a goal yet.
- You want to meet with people who will generate ideas.

CHECKLIST FOR BOARD MEMBER MEETINGS

BEFORE THE MEETING

- Research the potential board member's history.
- What is unique about this person?
- What is it about his or her story that you want to understand more about?
- Come up with a list of questions to ask. You need information about every aspect of your profession, types of continuing education, current pay for varied roles, general trends, and future outlook.

AT THE MEETING

- Ask for referrals of other people who might be able to help you. Be clear that you want to widen your network. This is about people with whom you have synergy or who can help you sharpen your vision.
- What are you hoping to learn or gain from this person?

AFTER THE MEETING

- Take notes about what transpired during the meeting, such as decisions made, advice offered, and next steps.
- Review the focus of the meeting: you are trying to make some decisions about your career and fill yourself up with information that isn't already available.
- Review the reason you are making this list: you are thinking of people who interest you.
- Are you still interested in this person?
- Remember that it is a constantly growing list, always being updated.

CASE STUDIES OF BOARD
MEMBER MEETINGS

Diana has been a director at a non-profit foundation for the past eight years. She has held a variety of positions in this field. There are 20 other directors in her organization, and she is aware that the chief operations officer is about to retire at the end of next year.

She is interested in the job, but there are other people with more experience who would be more likely candidates. She wants to consult a board member about the best way to increase her chances of being awarded the position. Diana will review her board to find the appropriate member, then make of a list of questions to ask. She will then get a list of referrals and think about the actions she should take once she meets with them. She will need to find out what she needs to learn and get some additional education. How she approaches the board member meeting depends on a number of variables. First, the depth of her relationship with this person is key to what questions she needs to ask (for example, she know the person's story already) and the manner in which she mines for information. Diana needs to determine if this person can be helpful and to think about how she can be helpful back. The next important element for Diana—and for anyone—is to determine the purpose of the meeting, such as looking for a referral, seeking sponsorship in pursuit of a certain position, looking for a new job. The most important thing is to identify the purpose; you don't want to go to a meeting without having a clear purpose for it. Many times, the purpose is to pick a mentor's brain about some unique aspect of their role or the profession as a whole.

QUESTIONS FOR DIANA'S PROFESSIONAL GURU

1. Examine and present your story:
   - This is where I am right now in my profession.
   - These are my current struggles.
   - Please give me your feedback about how you perceive me.
   - What do you think I need to work on right now? What are my personal challenges in terms of my goal to become a COO?
   - What skill set do I need to develop to be a strong candidate for the COO position?
   - Who else do you think I need to know or talk to?
   - What skills will the ideal candidate possess?
   - What questions do you think I should ask during the interview?
   - Is there something that you think that I should stress during the interview that may give me an advantage?
   - Which of my assets do you feel might be most appealing to the interviewer?
   - Is there anything that you can tell me about the organization? Is there someone you think might know about the organization?
   - Can I reach out to you again if I have other questions before my interview?

2. Mine your mentor for his or her story:
   - Please tell me your story. How did you become a COO?
   - What pitfalls have you run into as a COO?
   - If you could redo how you entered your role as a COO, what would you do differently?

CASE 2: VOLUNTEERING AS A MEANS TO AN END

It is often valuable to pursue opportunities that do not carry a larger title or extra income as a steppingstone to your goals. Volunteer for a role that addresses an organizational need, especially if it fits with your career plan. Even if there is no clear financial benefit, you will be gaining experience, connections, and visibility.

Imagine that you are working in a school setting, and the liaison between the mental health clinic team and the school is resigning in a month. It is a small team: four social workers and a supervisor. You are interested in the liaison role. You want to figure out how best to position yourself for the role, and you want to talk to your supervisor about it; the role does not carry a salary increase or a title change, just more exposure and opportunity. How do you use your board to do that? Have meetings with people who have given you encouragement in the past. Before the meeting with your supervisor, think about what makes you a good candidate, and get some feedback from other people about the following:

- The right timing—when you should approach your supervisor.
- How you should prepare for the meeting with your supervisor.
- The case for choosing you versus another candidate.
- How to assess your performance in your current role.
- Evidence that you are doing a good job.
- Brainstorming the argument that this won't interfere with your primary job responsibilities.
- Opinion about your suitability for the role.
- What qualities the supervisor seeks for this role.
- Determine if your résumé need to be reworked.
- Whom you can meet to learn how you can contribute to this role.
- Whether you can meet with the outgoing employee so you can better understand the position.
- Brainstorming ideas on how to increase the functioning of the role.

Remember, you are approaching the supervisor to make a case for why he or she should consider you for this role. You are informing the decision maker that, in no uncertain terms, you are more than just interested in this role—you are proactively pursuing the position. This type of ambitious, go-getter attitude is very impressive to decision makers and supervisors and will go a long way to make you stand out from the crowd.

KEEPING IN TOUCH WITH
BOARD MEMBERS

If you believe business is built on relationships, make building them your business.

Scott Stratten

Keep in touch with your potential board members. Even if they do not become board members, you should keep in touch with these people for the purpose of being able to use them as referral sources for somebody else who may need a mentor or for a future need. This process is not quick, and it will not happen overnight, but as time goes on, it will develop. The goal is to find your true calling. Remember that you are not actually asking people to serve on your board; the board is a mental construct, and members will not know that they are serving on your board.

Just because one person isn't right for your board, this doesn't mean that you forget about them. He or she may have contacts or resources that may be helpful or may be more appropriate for a colleague's board instead, and you may gift that person a recommendation. Moreover, he or she could evolve into the type of person who will fit into a later configuration of your board, as your vision expands and especially if you change your career trajectory. So it is not recommended to dismiss a potential board member out of hand simply because he or she does not fulfill a role right now.

Your board should include people at all levels of your organization and in your profession. You need connections with people who are new to the profession and people who have a lower role than you in your organization, such as mailroom personnel, maintenance staff, clerical workers, or peers in another department. Connections of all sorts are helpful in expanding your influence. One of my coaching clients got a prize appointment to a sought-after corporate board as a result of a connection made by the security guard at her office. He was the Little League coach for the son of the board's chairperson.

In her book *Expect to Win: 10 Proven Strategies for Thriving in the Workplace*, Carla Harris talks about the need to recognize the power of everyone in the network. She especially points out the power held by assistants, which highlights their value as gatekeepers:

> Another type of relationship vital to your professional network is your relationship with the assistants of those people who are senior to you. The assistants are the ultimate gatekeepers. I have seen so many people derail themselves by ignoring, or worse yet, being rude to a senior person's assistant. They failed to recognize how important this person could be in their network of relationships. . . . Everyone has power, and that power is to be honored in everyone in your network.
>
> In most professional organizations, the person closest to the CEO, CFO, or COO is their assistant. Not only can the assistant get you access to the senior person, but they also can give you information about how intense their day was, what their mood might be, the best way to approach them, when to approach them, and so on. The assistant can set the context of your conversation, so that whatever

you need to approach them with will be perceived in the best possible light. I cannot count the number of times I needed access to an extraordinarily busy, senior person who in the normal course of business would have considered me to be low on their priority list. Normally I wouldn't be able to get an appointment for a very long time. But because I had fostered a good relationship with that person's assistant, I was squeezed in to see them, often on the very same day I requested a few minutes of their time.

Harris, 2009, p. 186

Harris also highlights very powerful examples of gifting through her interactions with the assistants within her organization:

How did I build some of my assistant relationships? By taking advantage of the opportunities that I had to interact with them: for example, when I was waiting outside of a senior person's office, at Christmas parties, in the cafeteria, or any place that I had an opportunity to chat with them. In most cases, they are women just like me, so we already have a lot in common to talk about. I also have been helpful on career day at their children's schools when they wanted a banker to come in and talk. I would make myself available to discuss college or music with their children, or if they needed help or a word of encouragement in their own professional development. You never know what you have to offer someone else and how that offer may be useful to you down the road as a part of the reciprocation in a relationship. When I offered myself to help them, I was not looking for something in return; it was the fact that I was willing to be of service in our relationship that it came back to benefit me later.

Harris, 2009, p. 186

WORKING WITH YOUR BOARD

Board members gain pleasure from witnessing your growth and seeing their connections pay off for you. Offering you guidance allows board members to enhance their coaching and leadership talents. Sharing their wisdom with you inspires board members to step up their own game to an even higher level. Being on your board strengthens their expertise and positions as go-to persons in the profession. Some board members should be people who have had similar experiences in their career and are further along in their professional journey than you. You want to learn about their challenges and how they overcame obstacles.

Relationships take time to grow, so make sure he or she is a trusted board member before you share too much. As time passes and the relationship grows strong, you can share more. The aim is that the relationship is never superficial, is always authentic, and deepens with time.

Share your fears, challenges, and limitations with your mentors no matter how embarrassing. Likewise, you should also share your professional aspirations with board members no matter how big or lofty—or impossible—they may seem to you.

Make notes about action items, and follow through. Being consistent with follow-up is a major key to success. Be creative in helping your board members know that you value them and their time. Make sure that your board members know about the successes you derived from their counsel. Do not hesitate to share your wisdom and resources regardless of the power difference. What you bring to the table is of value. Don't withhold your treasures because of your insecurities or your junior status.

Gifting to mentors is a simple yet crucial element of a symbiotic mentor-mentee relationship. You must make board members feel valued and appreciated by taking the time out to get to know their work. This could be something as simple as keeping up with their blogs, making thoughtful comments on articles, and inspiring additional dialogue among colleagues by sharing a link on your Facebook or LinkedIn profile. Gift items that are meaningful and that you can easily afford. Never gift items that require a board member to spend private time with you in order to accept them. A gift should never be self-serving. Handwritten cards, information about a conference, links to a new book, resources that were distributed at a conference, and referrals are all small and unexpected gifts that are appropriate throughout the year. Gifting is a two-way street. It can include sharing information about events, recommending a particular article, or buying a box of someone's favorite tea.

In *Managers as Mentors: Building Partnerships for Learning*, Chip R. Bell and Marshall Goldsmith describe gifting as follows:

> Gifting is the act of generosity. Gifting, as opposed to giving, means bestowing something of value upon another without expecting anything in return. Mentors have many gifts to share. When they bestow those gifts abundantly and unconditionally, they strengthen the relationship and keep it healthy. Gifting is the antithesis of taking or using manipulatively. It is at the opposite end of the spectrum from greed. Gifting is often seen as the main event of mentoring. Mentors gift advice, they gift feedback, they gift focus and direction, they gift the proper balance between intervening and letting protégés test their wings, and they gift their passion for learning. Surrendering and accepting are important initial steps in creating a readiness in the protégé. Gifts are wasted when they are not valued—when they are discounted and discarded.
>
> Bell & Goldsmith, *2013, p. 33*

POSITIVE QUALITIES TO SEEK IN YOUR BOARD MEMBERS

People inspire you, or they drain you—pick them wisely.

Hans F Hansen

- Enthusiastic, with a zest for life, making contributions to their profession.
- Passionate and dedicated to their position.
- Knowledgeable about their field.
- Accessible and available to be a resource.
- Possessing unique qualities that you can draw on.
- Open and able to share their knowledge and experience.
- Satisfied with their career and professionally successful.
- Generous in spirit, thoughtful, perceptive, and intuitive.
- Friendly and outgoing (so they have a large network of contacts).
- With a can-do attitude, confident, believing in themselves.
- Interested in you, someone you have synergy with.
- Functioning as connectors.
- Nourishing your dreams and feeding your spirit.
- Functioning as keepers of the dream.
- Offering you encouragement.
- Giving you straight talk, no chaser.
- Genuinely caring and empathetic.
- Possessing excellent crisis-management skills.
- Politically savvy.
- Highly regarded.
- Seen as go-to persons.
- Regarded as industry thought leaders.

NEGATIVE QUALITIES TO AVOID IN YOUR BOARD MEMBERS

> Negative people are like two-ton anchors. They weigh you down and prevent you from going anywhere.
>
> Jerry Bruckner

You don't want any board members who have a negative attitude or bad energy. As soon as you witness a potential board member exhibit any of the following behaviors, eliminate him or her as a possible mentor. You should always trust your gut instincts when it comes to evaluating whether or not an individual is right for your board, but look out for the following red flags that indicate that someone is not right for your board.

- Naysayers who tend to drag other people down.
- Constantly complaining about their jobs, life, society, or other people.
- Hopeless about potential accomplishment for the future.
- Bitter or unfulfilled in their career.
- Talking about others behind their backs or gossiping.
- Unable to be trusted or to honor confidentiality.
- Unreliable or unavailable (emotionally or physically).
- Unscrupulous, unethical, or immoral.
- Irresponsible with practical matters.
- Self-destructive.
- Functioning as spirit robbers and dream killers.
- Insecure.
- Uninterested in instilling confidence in others.
- Focused on taking more than giving.
- Continuously seeking acknowledgment and validation.
- Belittling of you or your dreams.
- Taking credit for your work, the work of the team, or the work of others.

Be especially careful not to get stuck doing tasks or projects from which you do not learn new skills or in which you cannot see value to your professional development. VPBOD interactions by definition tend to be short-term in nature. Long-term assignments require financial compensation for mentor or mentee. Get a quick check, or consult with your SWAT Team before accepting a long-term assignment for a board member; while most board members are likely to be ethical and considerate, they are still human and may be capable of taking advantage. It is your responsibility to look out for yourself, and consulting a board member is just one way you can do so.

WORKSHEET: CONFIRMED BOARD MEMBER LIST

This list includes names of people you will add to your board after an initial meeting; their specialties, titles, and organizations; their feedback about you; and what slots on the board they can fill.

Mentor Name	Title, Company	Board Office	Top Quality	Referrals	Resources	Connections	Follow-up Items

YOUR PROFESSIONAL VISION

Vision is the art of seeing the invisible.

Jonathan Swift

After the board-building process is under way, your objectives are starting to become defined, as are the individual goals leading toward those objectives. By the time your board is established, you should have a fully formed vision of your best self and your professional future. Your "professional vision quest" is the process of achieving a coherent, clear, and well-defined future for your career and your professional identity. There are a number of exercises you may do in order to assist you in your vision questing:

1. At the end of your initial board-building process, once you have identified and defined your first Personal Board of Directors, you begin formulating your professional vision, using potential and current board member meetings, advice, and knowledge to clarify your original goals and objectives. Remember, one of the fundamental purposes of building and maintaining a VPBOD is to achieve clarity of your vision of your future career.

2. Create a vision statement that encapsulates your *current* vision of your career future. You should come up with a name for your vision quest, such as "Maria's Triumphant Return to Management" or "Karine Is Promoted to Senior Executive Vice President" or "Tonia Is Awarded Her PhD in Social Work."

3. Next, come up with a narrative that describes the process of realizing that vision. Envision it as a story you tell in the future after you have already accomplished it. Draw on the various objectives and goals outlined in chapter 5 as points in the plot and action. Use your board members as characters in the story, and if appropriate, include colleagues and role models you envision playing a part and reflect on how they guide and advise you along your journey.

4. Draw up the vision statement, of no more than two sentences, that summarizes and communicates your vision. This statement is your **elevator speech**; you should be able to communicate it to someone in the typical time an elevator ride takes. You can use this vision statement throughout your professional networking as a short, pithy description of your professional vision, which you can share with potential board members or connections.

5. Create a "vision board," or a visual collage, where you can assemble images that spark your vision and stimulate your creativity. If you are trying to create and brand a product, you should put mock-ups of the logo and packaging on your vision board. Have a mock newspaper story printed up, with the headline describing the ultimate vision of your future career: "Brian Lee is appointed Chief of Police of the N.J. State Police." Hang your vision board in your home office or wherever you spend time working at home. A simple corkboard equipped with push pins will do, but you can make it however you want. Assemble images, perhaps clippings from magazines, perhaps motivational affirmations, sketches, and diagrams, anything that gets you thinking about your vision in tangible, concrete terms. The goal of your vision board is to make your vision real and to

think about your vision every time you glance at it. You can use images that have significance only to you, that carry certain private associations, that prompt reflection about something related to your vision. Your vision board will change and evolve with you as you progress along your path and as your vision becomes more and more clear. You will see your vision developing right before your eyes, and the narrative of your vision will shift accordingly, as will your objectives and goals.

6. Come up with a communication plan for explaining your vision to others, akin to a sales pitch. You must be able to communicate your vision succinctly and accurately in order to discuss it with your board members and receive the proper feedback, guidance, and knowledge along the way. Your board members may be able to introduce you to the mavens and connectors who can help you achieve your vision. These discussions will also help you vet your vision for unreasonable or off-track goals, in addition to refining and clarifying your vision.

Remember, you don't start with a vision. You create a vision as a result of the initial self-reflection and goal setting we did in chapter 4 and then through the process of board building we did in chapter 5, both of which were designed to help you achieve clarity about not only your objectives but also about who you are through advice, feedback, and knowledge. Board members are also role models who inspire and motivate you. Even potential board members who don't make the cut contribute to your attainment of clarity by helping you identify those things you do *not* want to do or pursue. By the time you have built the first iteration of your VPBOD, you should have a very clear vision of the future of your career. And even though your vision will constantly change and evolve, you must create this vision in order to let it grow. You can set goals to accomplish objectives without having a clear vision, but doing so could be a robotic, uninspired process that ends up for naught. Your professional vision synthesizes your previous work—seeking out and meeting with board members, getting their advice and feedback, reflecting, and establishing your own identity—and is the product of and perpetuates passion, commitment, clarity, and ambition. Without vision, your career goals are likely to become nebulous and quickly lose cohesion, and your progress will not gain any momentum because you lack the inspiration and motivation that fuel your desire to achieve your goals and objectives en route to realizing your ultimate vision. Without a long-term vision, it is hard to discern the path right in front of you, and your career journey could become a maze, a series of incorrect choices; you could find yourself in a rut, or you could accomplish objectives surely and steadily but without enthusiasm or passion, ending up in a place professionally that may represent success and achievement to the outside world but does not stimulate you or make you happy.

Vision is essential to becoming your best self. At some point in your journey toward the achievement of your vision, you will eventually reach a tipping point, where everything just seems to fall into place, when synchronicity dominates and everything becomes easy. You seem to meet the exact right connections exactly when you need them, you are so good at your job that it becomes a pleasure to go to work every day, you find yourself advancing up the ladder at breakneck speed, and you receive professional awards and recognition for your excellent performance. As you grow and leverage your board, this snowball effect will kick in, and when this happens, you will know your vision is close on the horizon.

FAMOUS MENTORING PAIRS: POLITICS II

Mentor	Mentee
Derry Irvine, Baron Irvine of Lairg, UK lord high chancellor	Tony Blair, UK prime minister
Lyndon B. Johnson, US president	John Connally, US secretary of the treasury
John F. Kennedy, US president	Rey A. Carr, founder and CEO of Peer Resources
Richard Nixon, US president	George W. Bush, US president
Charles J. Ogletree, Harvard law professor	Barack Obama, US president
Thomas Pendergast, political activist	Harry S. Truman, US president
William Ravenel, high school teacher	John McCain, US senator
Eleanor Roosevelt, US first lady and human rights activist	Hillary Clinton, US first lady and secretary of state
Theodore Roosevelt, US president	William Howard Taft, US president
Joseph Stalin, Soviet leader	Nikita Khrushchev, Soviet premier
Cyrus Vance, US secretary of state	Warren Christopher, US secretary of state
Thurlow Weed, founder of the Whig Party	Millard Fillmore, US president

PROFILES IN MENTORSHIP: HILLARY CLINTON AND ELEANOR ROOSEVELT

Author Bob Woodward claimed in his 1996 book *The Choice* that Hillary Clinton (figure 6.2) engaged in imaginary conversations with Eleanor Roosevelt (figure 6.3) and also with Mahatma Gandhi as a therapeutic exercise. And while she was campaigning for president in 2007, Clinton said she found inspiration in the words of Roosevelt.

FIGURE 6.2 Mentee: Hillary Clinton, former US first lady and secretary of state.

FIGURE 6.3 Mentor: Eleanor Roosevelt, former US first lady and human rights activist.

"She said, 'You know, if you're going to be involved in politics you have to grow skin as thick as a rhinoceros,'" Clinton told an audience of female political activists, as reported in the *New York Daily News*.

"So occasionally, I'll be sitting somewhere and I'll be listening to someone perhaps not saying the kindest things about me. And I'll look down at my hand and I'll sort of pinch my skin to make sure it still has the requisite thickness I know Eleanor Roosevelt expects me to have," she said.

QUOTES FROM ELEANOR ROOSEVELT

In 1936, Roosevelt summarized for women in public life what she had learned:

"You cannot take anything personally."

"You cannot bear grudges."

"You must finish the day's work when the day's work is done."

"You cannot get discouraged too easily."

"You have to take defeat over and over again and pick up and go on."

"Be sure of your facts."

"Argue the other side with a friend until you have found the answer to every point which might be brought up against you."

"Women who are willing to be leaders must stand out and be shot at. More and more they are going to do it, and more and more they should do it."

"Every woman in public life needs to develop skin as tough as rhinoceros hide."

"Women are like tea bags. You never know how strong they are until they get into hot water."

KNOWLEDGE NUGGETS

- Crafting your Virtual Personal Board of Directors requires careful planning, conscious effort, and calculated thought.
- The main reason for maintaining a Personal Board is to become your best self, both personally and professionally.
- You must prospect for board members in the usual places, such as where you work or go to school, and also in unusual places, because you never know where you might meet a board member.
- You must prepare for meetings with prospective mentors thoroughly beforehand in order to make the most of your meetings.
- Getting referrals is one of the most important goals of board member meetings.
- When you appoint mentors to your Personal Board, remember that you do not extend a formal invitation, since your VPBOD is a mental construct.

CHAPTER 7

LEVERAGING YOUR PERSONAL BOARD

More business decisions occur over lunch and dinner than at any other
time, yet no MBA courses are given on the subject.

Peter Drucker

SO YOU HAVE A PERSONAL BOARD, NOW WHAT DO YOU DO?

GETTING TO KNOW YOUR BOARD MEMBERS: BUILDING RELATIONSHIPS

Once you have chosen specific members to staff your Virtual Personal Board of Directors, the next step is to get to know each board member in more depth. Once you decide to appoint a specific person to your board, you should try to have a one-on-one with that member. You might have a few public encounters with a board member; the goal is to plan to attend events where the person will be, such as receptions or workshops. Remind the person of where you met before, and interact with him or her so that you can arrange for a meeting at a later date.

At some point after you appoint someone to your board, you want to foster a situation in which you may have a face-to-face meeting in order to get acquainted with each other. However, do not force this meeting to happen; you want the meeting to occur at the right time (naturally), but it does not have to be immediately after you appoint the board member; it may not happen until a few months later. Until this happens, you should be researching the person, following what he or she is doing, and getting to know your new board member from afar, so that when you do have the first face-to-face, you can make the best impression and demonstrate that you are interested and engaged in his or her professional life. This will enable you to have more meaningful conversations with the board member, have well-thought-out questions to ask, and have ways to foster collaboration and further interaction. Remember, one of the main goals of this meeting is to endear you to the board member and make him or her want to continue to build the relationship and deepen the bond.

It is preferable to allow board members to choose the time and location for the one-on-one so they feel most comfortable and so it is most convenient for them. You do not want to take board members out of their element or cause them to make a sacrifice or lose time in order to meet with you. Most board members don't need you to take them to dinner; you do not want to infringe upon their very valuable personal time. This does not mean that you can't go to dinner, but it it is not a perk or a gift for board members to have you take them to dinner, since it takes time away from their personal lives. Have dinner only if they suggest it. It is best to think of interactions with board members as being a part of the workday/week, so stay away from evenings and weekends—except if a board member suggests it.

You want to make it as easy as possible. A board member may want meetings to take place in his or her office. Meeting settings should be quiet places that make communication easy. Such face-to-face meetings could be afternoon tea or coffee, breakfast before work, a lunch meeting (only if the board member suggests it), or a cocktail right after work. You want to follow their lead and let them decide where and when to meet you.

Always offer to pay the tab. While many senior board members may offer to put the bill on their expense accounts, you should offer and never suggest a place where you cannot afford to pay the bill. Most board members are likely not to suggest a high-end meeting place unless they plan to pay. Incorporate the cost of networking into your budget. It is an investment in your career.

Remember, spending one-on-one time with your board members is not easy, because they are in high demand and are very busy, but it is very important that you do spend this one-on-one time. You want to finesse a situation in which a one-on-one meeting is a naturally occurring development. For example, you attend a workshop conference at which a board member is speaking and make an insightful comment afterward that may interest the board member so much that he or she suggests the one-on-one; as rare as this may be, it is the ideal way for a one-on-one to occur.

Although you may have already become very familiar with a board member's professional work in a public sense, during the one-on-one, you are trying to discover who this person really is and to get to know him or her better. You want to establish a personal connection with but not an intimate one. The goal is not to make this person your friend. You want to deepen your professional relationship by getting to know things that are not public knowledge and that clue you in to areas you can later leverage to deepen your connection even further. At this one-on-one, you want to find out what the board member's specialty area is in the profession. You might think you know it already, but there is always something you don't know about a person. You need to find out what your board members' passions are, who their connections are, what organizations they belong to, what their other areas of interest are, and what is unique about them. Aside from professional qualities, you should also try to discover personal interests such as hobbies and so that you may engage them. By locating commonalities that you may share, you will deepen your connection.

At the one-on-one, you want to paint a well-rounded picture of who you are. There are certain topics you will touch on, but most of these qualities that you want to communicate to your board members will become a continuing conversation throughout your relationship. However, at the introductory one-on-one, it is important that you touch on all of these topics so that board members can understand you and be able to best assist you.

Talk about your family, talk about your background, discuss your friends and associates, and discuss your professional accomplishments. You want to tailor the information you share to your concept of what they are going to be most interested in and who they are. You don't want to air your dirty laundry or discuss inappropriate intimate subjects. Keep the conversation light and positive and oriented toward subjects that the board members are associated with. You may want to think strategically beforehand about exactly the types of information about yourself that you want a specific board member to know about. Remember, first impressions are very important, and you want to make the best impression on your new board member at this meeting.

Another safe area of conversation is to communicate current events in your life, such as the fact that you just started bicycling, that you are renovating your house, or that you are learning a new musical instrument. The idea here is that you are sharing information that paints a picture of who you are so that your board members can get to know the real you in more depth and help establish you as a real person in their eyes. This enables board members to understand where you are in your life and characterize who you are in terms of demographics—a new mother, a recently married person, or getting close to retirement. This will enable them to be more helpful to you and give you information that is more useful to you as an individual. For example, a board member might find out about a parenting group for new mothers that he or she can suggest to you because the board member knows that you are a new mother.

You also should have a spiel that you tell every board member, a kind of verbal résumé that summarizes your professional situation, your aspirations, and issues you are challenged by. It is especially important that you share professional challenges that you are experiencing with which a specific board member would be particularly suited to help you with. You could talk about the challenges of working in private practice, for a large or a small organization, with new professionals, issues associated with frequent travel, or being the youngest or oldest person on a team. Try to choose challenges that you both might share.

Another way to help your board members get to know you is to share your loftiest aspirations. It is important to be open and honest with new board members. Do not be embarrassed to admit exactly what your dreams are for your professional future even if they seem to you like a major stretch. Consider the fact that your potential mentors started *somewhere*, and they know what it is like to have big dreams, so they are not likely to look down on you for maintaining grand goals for your own future. Les Brown said, "Shoot for the moon; even if you miss, you'll fall in the stars." So whatever it is you want to do, go for it.

Your board members will be able to help you most efficiently if you are honest about exactly what you want to achieve. This way, they can be on the lookout for information that will help you and also think about forging connections that will guide you on your path to achieving your goals. You introduce this aspect of yourself at the one-on-one, but it is a developing conversation. Be mindful about oversharing in the early meetings; you want to share enough so that the person knows who you are but wait until the relationship and trust develop before you share too deeply. These conversations are usually reserved for people outside of your organization. It's unwise to discuss your goals that do not pertain to your organization with people in your organization unless the relationship is solid.

When you share your loftiest aspirations, your mentors may help you broaden your dreams. They will point you in a direction that will lead to accomplishing these dreams by suggesting interim steps along the way that you may not have considered or realized. They can also put you in the company of people who have already achieved the goals that you have, and they can provide role models you can emulate to help you clarify your vision of how to accomplish these dreams. Your board members will be able to encourage you and help you to realize that it is possible for you to accomplish this dream; they can help you feel that it is real and possible. It is necessary that you believe in yourself, and when a mentor believes in you, it can help to build you confidence. Mentors can also help you strategize and suggest activities that will enable you to achieve these dreams.

> A mentor is someone who sees more talent and ability within you than you see in yourself, and helps bring it out of you.
>
> Bob Proctor

You can share your deepest fears and anxieties with your board members at your one-on-one and throughout your relationship. You want to be able to work through these fears and have your board members help you. For example, a mentee has a fear of speaking in public. Her mentor suggests that she attend a workshop on public speaking and pushes her to present at several conferences in order to confront this fear. Your board members give you access to opportunities you otherwise wouldn't have and encourage you to take advantage of these opportunities. Board members can push you and challenge you to deal with and overcome this fear. People are often resistant and avoid confronting their fears, so if you have people to encourage you along the way, it will be easier, and they will hold you accountable to making progress and really making an effort to overcome this fear. Also, you have someone who can provide emotional support about this fear and with whom you can openly discuss it without embarrassment or making yourself vulnerable. Your mentor is a safe person on whom you can lean. Discussing your fears is one of the first steps to overcoming them. And having someone to support you and encourage you is very important. Your mentors can also share their own fears so that you realize that everybody has them. They can share their experiences and how they overcame their obstacles. This can help you to feel less isolated, and you may be inspired by their stories.

> There's fear that keeps you alive. And there's fear that keeps you from living. Wisdom is knowing the difference.
>
> David Swenson

WHEN SHOULD YOU ASK A BOARD MEMBER FOR HELP?

You should always be seeking knowledge nuggets from your board members about their current views and a future forecast for the profession. However, there are many situations throughout your career when you should consult your VPBOD to address specific issues. The advice of a trusted board member could improve and inform your decision-making process. The following is a brief list of situations we all face in our personal and professional lives.

JOB-RELATED

- Looking for a new job.
- Having a struggle with a boss or a coworker.
- Being overlooked or passed over for a promotion or open position.
- Needing to decide between two job offers.
- Brainstorming ideas for additional income streams.

- Needing to choose whether to relocate for a job.
- Thinking about changing your career direction.
- Being asked by the organization to take on an assignment that was not in your career plan.
- Handling a mistake that is affecting your career.
- Receiving negative micro-messages.
- Handling a disrespectful senior executive in your organization.

BIG DECISIONS

- Thinking about taking a maternity or paternity leave.
- Thinking about having a baby.
- Thinking about taking a leave of absence.
- Evaluating a higher-paying job offer or a job that is not on your intended career path.
- Evaluating a promotion offer that requires relocation or significant travel.

ETHICAL ISSUES

- Dealing with a supervisor who wants you to do something unethical or illegal.
- Responding when fraud, such as Medicaid fraud, is being investigated and an investigator wants to talk to you about it.
- Handling sexual harassment issues—you or a coworker being investigated for sexual harassment or similar misconduct.
- Dealing with misconduct by a supervisor or subordinate.
- Preparing to testify for court-related issues.
- Dealing with issues that you believe reflect bias toward you or others.

REFERRALS AND INFORMATION

- Mining for information about somebody who may be a future coworker or potential supervisor.
- Seeking an organization or agency that you are considering joining.
- Seeking sponsorship for a position on a board.
- Preparing for a job interview.
- Determining the skills necessary for a desired position.
- Seeking an introduction to a desired connection.

EXPERT OPINION

- Deciding whether to go back to school.
- Responding when someone appropriates your idea at work.
- Responding to negative feedback or evaluation.

- Handling a bully at work.
- Getting feedback about how you are perceived.
- Understanding and navigating office politics and answering questions such as whether you should take sides or stay neutral in a dispute between a coworker and your boss.
- Recovering from a mistake, big or small.
- Assessing a volunteer assignment for career value.
- Evaluating job offers beyond their financial value.

SUBCOMMITTEES OF YOUR PERSONAL BOARD

By arranging your VPBOD members into subcommittees, you will be able to maximize the efficiency with which you can access their guidance. Remember, the VPBOD is virtual: the Swat Team, the Executive Committee, and the Diversity & Equity Committee members are not meeting or consulting as a group. You individually consult each member and then synthesize all recommendations in order to formulate your own decision. Subcommittees are especially useful for addressing short-term issues that occur during the course of your day-to-day work life. They are helpful when you need a quick turnaround on a pressing question or issue. One-minute mentoring and the quick check are other techniques you can employ when you need a fast consultation with a board member; as was detailed earlier in chapter 2.

SWAT TEAM

The acronym SWAT stands for "Special Weapons and Tactics" and is a term first coined for use by the Los Angeles police force's special response unit, which was equipped to handle any emergency, however bizarre or unusual, at a moment's notice, with the highest level of expertise, precision, and proficiency. Likewise, your Personal Board's SWAT Team is a special team of board members made up of capable, accomplished individuals on whom you can depend for the most serious crises that may arise on the job. Your SWAT Team is assembled when a mission-critical issue needs immediate attention from a group of hand-picked specialists in specific areas related to your particular emergency.

When you have a pressing matter, such as a job offer you need to respond to by morning, you can rely on your SWAT Team for not only a quick but also an informed response. The composition of the SWAT Team will change all the time depending on the nature of the particular emergency you are dealing with. The most important element of the SWAT Team is that each member is available, is interested in you, can maintain confidentiality, and has judgment you trust. There are different levels of SWAT needs. Sometimes issues are career-threatening, and at other times, the wrong decisions will affect the flow of your daily life. There are emergencies with a big E and with a little e. If it is a little-e issue, you might not need the Chairperson; you may just want to refer to a second- or third-string board member. When dealing with a big-E emergency, you should always try to get at least two or three different responses and compare opinions. Sometimes a combination of answers is what you need rather than one definitive conclusion. Keep in mind that you are going to use the combined wisdom of the board to come up with the best solution. You are always the final decision maker.

EXECUTIVE COMMITTEE

The Executive Committee, also known as the Kitchen Cabinet, is your most trusted group of advisors. The Executive Committee is the group of people whose opinions you pool together when you have a crucial decision to make that requires multiple points of view. These are the people who know your overall goals, skills, and experience. In other words, they know *you*—the real you—so they can give you informed opinions and wise observations; they are like-minded and exhibit a professional temperament similar to your own. You should use your Executive Committee to have your meeting-before-the-meeting when considering important, career-changing decisions. These are the board members you run these important decisions by in order to solidify your own thinking on important issues. The number of people on your Executive Committee will grow and change depending on your current situation and as you build your VPBOD over the course of your career.

DIVERSITY & EQUITY COMMITTEE

A committee for Diversity & Equity can point out where you may be playing into stereotypes others may have regarding you and offer suggestions to help mitigate those messages in your public communications. Sarah, a 35-year-old white director of an outpatient mental health clinic in a predominantly Latino community, had to hire a new employee for a supervisor opening. She needed help choosing between a white male with 12 years of experience and a Latina with eight years of experience. Because her coworkers and employees had previously criticized the lack of diversity on her team, she decided to consult her Diversity & Equity Committee for assistance in making this decision. Her D&E Committee consisted of a black woman who was a former colleague, a young Latina who was a past student of a class she taught, and a white man who held a directorship in a similar organization.

The feedback Sarah received from her D&E Committee completely changed her outlook about the supervisor position. Whereas she was leaning toward hiring the more experienced white male at first, after consulting her D&E Committee, Sarah decided to hire the Latina despite the fact that she had less time out of school. Sarah's former colleague, the black woman, explained that having a more diverse team positively affected staff retention. The young Latina committee member advised Sarah that hiring a Spanish-speaking supervisor from within the clinic community would be especially meaningful to the staff and local residents. In addition, the Latina's clinical input—enhanced by her "lived experience"—would enable the team to provide better services to their clients. The white male committee member explained that his own diversified team gave him access to different points of view that were crucial when making important decisions with regard to providing services to communities of color.

After consulting with her D&E team, Sarah realized that she felt more comfortable with a leadership team whose members were more like her. Sarah's D&E Committee helped her face the fact that she needed to step outside her comfort zone when hiring employees to ensure that she was maintaining a leadership staff that more closely represented the population they served. This is why you need a committee for Diversity & Equity: no one individual can provide all of the different viewpoints needed for a well-rounded perspective on sensitive political issues such as race or unintentional bias.

CASE STUDY: LEVERAGING YOUR BOARD'S DIVERSITY & EQUITY COMMITTEE

Carlos, 40, a unit director at a residential facility, was a single, physically attractive man of color who supervised a staff of mostly women of color. There were three other men who worked on the unit, all of whom were white. Carlos was uneasy about closing his office door when meeting with a female staff member. However, he did conduct closed-door meetings with his male staffers and socialized with them at lunch and after work hours in order to cultivate professional relationships. Carlos was not comfortable socializing with female staffers outside the office because he was concerned that they would assume that he was making sexual advances. Two of his female supervisees had flirted with him, and a female coworker had asked him out on a date. He had declined based on his no-dating-at-work policy, and it had negatively affected their working relationship. Although his intention was to protect his reputation, his actions resulted in female staff members complaining that he favored the males. Additionally, since the men with whom he socialized were white and the women who felt rejected were of color, rumors started that he was attempting to gain the favor of the white people in the agency and believed himself to be "too good" to socialize with other people of color. Carlos needed advice about how to deal with his female staff and coworkers fairly, how to handle cases of sexual attraction at the workplace, and, finally, how to respond to questions and tensions around race.

Carlos drew up a subcommittee from his Personal Board consisting of an older man of color, a single woman of color, and a married white woman. He was then able to talk to them about his concerns and feelings of vulnerability in terms of his relationships with single women, both white women and women of color. He also talked with them about his relationships with the men on his unit and the issues of authority that arose with a man of color supervising and mentoring white men. Through these discussions, Carlos realized that his desire to socialize with the men was motivated by wanting to neutralize the tensions around authority; he was essentially looking for "male bonding" to diffuse some tension he did not know how to address.

The older man of color on Carlos's subcommittee had dealt with similar issues in his professional life. His advice was to treat women and men exactly the same in terms of closing the door during meetings and going out to lunch. He helped Carlos think through some of his own assumptions about race and gender that added to his insecurity and got in the way of his ability to handle subtle tensions head-on. Carlos consulted with the women on his subcommittee about the do's and don'ts of dealing with female coworkers professionally, from a *woman's* point of view. They shared their experiences and perceptions of how women interact professionally with men of color, and they helped clarify some of the issues around race. Carlos began to understand that the attraction he sensed from some of the women on his staff might not be sexual, per se, but might be an expression of admiration for him as a strong man of color and an expectation of camaraderie based on shared cultural heritage. Both subcommittee members advised him that he should make it known that he did not date at work as a matter of personal policy—no exceptions—in order to prevent potentially awkward situations.

Carlos gleaned from the advice of the team that he should limit his interactions with men and institute a policy with regard to socializing outside the workplace so everyone would be on the same page and he could manage expectations. The woman of color on his board suggested that Carlos speak to the woman he had declined a date with in order to address her issues directly and improve their working relationship. Because he was worried about what his boss would think about these issues, she suggested that he consult with his supervisor to update him on the problems and exactly what he was doing to solve them.

Ultimately, Carlos's relationships with his staff significantly improved after he implemented the advice of his diversity committee. Every other month, Carlos invited his entire staff—men and women—to a departmental lunch off-site. Doing so fostered a sense of camaraderie and greatly improved the workplace atmosphere for all parties involved

RULES OF ENGAGEMENT: HOW TO INTERACT WITH BOARD MEMBERS

There are Rules of Engagement for interacting with the members of your Personal Board on an ongoing basis. Remember, you use your board in a nonlinear fashion; you can be dealing with multiple issues simultaneously and consulting with a number of board members at any given time. The main goal is not to overwhelm any one board member with too many issues at once or demand too much of his or her time. For example, you may be asking three or four board members for advice about interviewing for a new job you want but at the same time have a SWAT Team assembled to address a pressing political issue at your current job. As a mentee, you may have multiple issues happening all at once, and you should consult with your mentors about all of them. And choosing the most appropriate and qualified board member from each office's roster is of the utmost importance in leveraging your board to the fullest extent.

MAINTAINING BOUNDARIES
WITH BOARD MEMBERS

You are not trying to make a friend; you have to treat a board member as a colleague and maintain professional boundaries. Occasionally, a board member may grow into a friend, but that is not the goal of the relationship. You are not inviting board members to your birthday parties; you are not socializing with your board members. It is burdensome and taxing for board members to decline inappropriate invitations, and this may cause them to withdraw.

But you might invite board members to an industry event that is in their field. You need to take the lead from the board member—pay attention to how interested the person is in you. You want to stay connected to each of your board members and have a running list of your interactions. Keep people's birthdays on your calendar, and send them a card every year. Keep their upcoming special events on your calendar, such as major speaking engagements or TV appearances, so that you can acknowledge them or check to see how they went with a quick e-mail or text. For example, if a board member is planning a first safari or a daughter's wedding or a spouse's surgery, let the person know that you value him or her and what matters to him or her. Always acknowledge any death, major illness, or loss.

GIFTING

Gifting is a two-way street: you are supporting your board members with the things they are doing, while they are helping you get where you want to go in your career. Gifting does not necessarily involve a physical item; it is more about going out of your way to support your board members. For example, if one of them is speaking at a conference, you would attend and bring some of your colleagues. If someone else you know is working on a similar project, you can connect them and make referrals regarding the things they are doing. Once in a while, there is a big gift, such as the referral of a coaching client or arranging a speaking engagement, but the main idea is understanding what the person is interested in, letting him or her know, and showing that you understand. If one of your mentors has just published a book, you would attend the book launch party, mention the book on your Facebook page, and encourage people to purchase and read it. Moreover, you could organize a group of people to all buy a mentor's eBook on the day it comes out, making it a bestseller in its category on Amazon.com. Doing things like this will show your board members that you are interested in the work they are doing. A gift like this that required so much effort on the mentee's part ended up motivating one mentor to begin sponsoring the mentee because she was so impressed and grateful for the tremendous amount of support for her book.

Board members also gift when it comes to their mentees. A mentor might pass on a helpful article to a protégé. A mentor could also invite a mentee to be an assistant at a conference he or she is holding. One of the most important things that a mentor does for a mentee is provide access to individuals and leverage his or her influence on the mentee's behalf. For example, the chief of staff of a congressman was able to gift his administrative assistant membership on a statewide taskforce on "The Barriers to Women in Leadership." The mentee contributed a section to the taskforce's position paper that greatly advanced her visibility in her field and, as a result, catapulted her into a more advanced career stage.

The important thing to remember about gifting, as mentioned, is that it is a two-way street. You should not think of it as a tit-for-tat type of process. You should make an effort to gift all your board members during your relationship whenever it is appropriate to do so. Sending e-mails (blind copy) with timely, interesting articles or links along with a short note—"I thought that you might find this interesting"—to board members is an easy way to offer a gift. This helps them to know that you are staying abreast of current events in the profession and thinking of them. Gifting is a major contributing factor that facilitates a mentor becoming a sponsor, not just a mentor, to a protégé in return for especially thoughtful and effective gifts. By giving special gifts to your mentor, you stand out from other mentees and get your board member's attention, which fosters a closer relationship and builds equity with the board member.

WHOM SHOULD YOU ASK FOR HELP?

Multiple board members are usually qualified to assist you and advise you on specific issue. Unless it is a matter requiring specialized knowledge and experience, such as a technological or legal issue, you should ask a few mentors for their opinions in order to have a variety to choose from, evaluate, and synthesize. Once you receive various opinions from different perspectives—remember, one of the goals of maintaining a VPBOD is to have access to different points of view—you should synthesize and evaluate their opinions in terms of your own preferences. You are not going to find one person who gives you the perfect answer; you will synthesize your own opinion from those that resonate with you. As you ask more and more questions of a variety of board members, you will gain clarity about your own positions on different issues and be able to make calls for yourself increasingly in the future. This process builds self-confidence and helps you construct your own professional identity, giving you a spectrum of choices and opinions on any one given issue to choose from. By aligning yourself with one or more opinions out of your various mentors' opinions, you are in the process of determining who you are and what your preferences are, thereby building your own professional identity.

When evaluating which board members to consult regarding a specific issue, it is wise to think about not only the content of the issue itself but also about how much time and effort you have been demanding from individual mentors recently. It is critical that you not depend too heavily on any one board member, as you will alienate that person by being too demanding and taking up too much of his or her time. You want to spread and distribute your time with your board members evenly among them. This is where your **mentor meeting journal** comes in handy. You should be noting each time you have an interaction with one of your mentors and keeping track of it so that you can review your recent activity and make the call on whether reaching out to him or her is appropriate at any given time.

You may also want to consider the various mentoring styles of your board members when choosing whom to ask for help on a particular issue.

WHEN TO TURN TO MORE THAN ONE BOARD MEMBER

You want several differing opinions from different types of people (e.g., someone who is new to the profession, someone in middle management, and a seasoned professional), so that you have a pool of information to choose from. The idea is to get a variety of ideas from different professional vantage points to aid you in your decision-making process.

BE YOUR BEST PROFESSIONAL SELF

You cannot be your best self by yourself. In order to be your best, you need to get information from a lot of different people. Listening to your instincts will help you figure out if something needs more work. Look for something that represents you that you can feel good about. Before your professional sense of self is fully developed, you are unsure. These consultations with board members develop your sense of professional confidence. The more you do it, the more of a sense of your professional self you will develop, and the less input you will need from others to feel confident. When you are newer at your job, you may need to get more feedback from others to reinforce your opinions. Speaking with board members is like practice for when you do have the big interview.

RULES OF ENGAGEMENT: KEEPING IN TOUCH WITH BOARD MEMBERS

SOCIAL MEDIA

Subscribe to board members' blogs, follow them on Twitter and LinkedIn, and attend online events, such as Livestream lectures they are appearing in, to demonstrate your interest in them and their work.

- Use e-mail, social media, and LinkedIn.
- Attend industry events that board members are involved in,
- Follow and participate in board members' blogs and websites.

E-MAIL

- Blind-copy all your board members when you send your e-mails. For example, you can say, "In case you didn't see this, I am featured in a magazine," and send it out to a bunch of your board members. Never send a group e-mail that shows the recipients' e-mail addresses.
- When sending mass e-mails, select a group of board members with whom you would like to develop deeper relationships and write a personalized introduction before sharing your news. The introduction should be a few sentences long. While time-consuming, it is well worth the investment.

PHONE

- Confirm with your board members their preferred modes of communication. Also pay attention to their communication patterns. Do they text, e-mails or phone most?
- Avoid writing long, convoluted e-mails. Be precise. Bullets, bullets, bullets. Most busy people have little tolerance for excessive details.
- Consult with your board members about which phone numbers to use and about leaving phone messages or messages with assistants. Many busy people have their messages screened, so confirming their preferences is best approach.
- As a rule of thumb, it is better not to leave detailed messages. Leave a very pleasant message with your number, but say that you will call again.
- If you speak with assistants, ask their opinion about how to reach your mentors.
- Make a point of being extra engaging with assistants; they will be the key to your getting a call back or your message delivered.
- Be specific about how much time you will need, such as "It is a quick conversation; I only need five minutes," or "I would like to set up a meeting for one hour."

YEAR IN REVIEW

Write up a "Year in Review" letter or e-mail to all of your board members annually. Draw up a standardized boilerplate letter that summarizes the activities and progress you made over the preceding year, with an emphasis on important accomplishments or awards and recognition. It is also good practice to personalize the letters or e-mails to a select group of board members with a sentence or two specifically about the recipient. Send these personalized e-mails to a select few board members who occupy a prime position on your board or with whom you would like to deepen your relationship. Then go into your own information. Send out an e-mail around the holidays or the new year. Be sure to thank your mentors for all their help during the past year. It is also a good time to remind them that you would be happy to be of assistance if they should need your help.

You do not have to include *every* mentor. Writing up a Year in Review letter is also a good practice that encourages reflection on the past year and taking a look at the big picture. It gives your board members the opportunity to hear about your past year's accomplishments and also what to expect for the coming year. And it holds you accountable for those goals in the upcoming year.

MIDYEAR UPDATE

It is optional, but you can also send another update e-mail or letter around the end of spring or midsummer, especially if you are having a banner year full of activities and accomplishments.

SAMPLE PERSONALIZED E-MAIL TO A MEMBER OF YOUR VPBOD

Dear Franklin,

Thank you so much for your words of encouragement. It really helped me get through the challenges of my new position as senior VP.

Below (and attached) is my Year in Review. It was such a great year, and so much of it was because of you. It would be a pleasure to provide you with any assistance in the coming year.

Thank you.
Jessica V.

JESSICA V. – YEAR IN REVIEW

November 30, 2014

What's Inside

- BIG ACCOMPLISHMENTS IN 2014
- ANNUAL SUMMARY OF ACTIVITIES
- EVENT FOR 2015
- HAPPY HOLIDAYS!

Big Accomplishments in 2014

This year has been a time of great opportunity, growth, and collaborations. I was promoted to Senior Vice President of Marketing at my firm in May. I co-wrote a book on public speaking called *Your Outdoor Voice: A how-to guide for public speaking*. Last month, I became a sponsor for one of the junior executives in my department. Looking forward to a banner year in 2015!!

Events for 2015

While 2014 was a very rewarding year; I'm looking forward to more challenges ahead:

- From January 12- March 30, I will be doing a national book tour for *Your Outdoor Voice: A how-to guide for public speaking*. Please check out our website www.youroutdoorvoice.com for more dates and locations.

- On April 4, I will host a networking event for junior professionals looking to build their Virtual Personal Board of Directors.

- I'm hosting a series of seminars for introverts on public speaking at NASW.

I was promoted to Senior Vice President of Marketing!

Annual Summary of Activities

- Running in the NYC Marathon in November.
- Raising $50,000 as fundraising chair for the local breast cancer nonprofit organization.
- Booking speaking engagements on motivational speaking, public relations, and social media for TEDTalks.
- Co-writing a new book on public speaking with Michelle D. called *Your Outdoor Voice: A how-to guide for public speaking*.

Happy Holidays!

During this holiday season, I hope you and your loved ones have peace, love, and fullfillment. I would like to wish you a joyous holiday season.

FIGURE 7.1 A sample Year in Review letter.

Develop an in-person schedule to connect with your board members over teas, lunches, or drinks. Keep a record to remind you of your board-nurturing activities.

MEETING FOR A PURPOSE
ANNUAL LUNCH

- This meeting is to catch up. It's an "in-person year in review" discussion of your vision for the coming year.
- Discuss added ambitions or big goals. Brainstorm shifts in direction—you might think of it as a brainstorming session to tweak your vision
- Get feedback and suggestions to evaluate and expand your vision and goals for the coming year.
- Discuss current trends and how they might influence your goals for the future.
- Catch up on personal social activities, such as past or planned travel.
- Share how your mentor's help has benefited you. Make it sort of a bragging session about your accomplishments.
- Be sure to spend time finding out what is going on for the mentor both personally and professionally. Ask what the mentor's plans are for the coming year.
- Develop a tradition, such as an annual lunch with your Chairperson(s), Professional Guru(s), or board members you are seeking to convert from mentors to sponsors.

CELEBRATORY EVENTS

Support your board members' celebrations:

- Attend book publication parties.
- Go to openings.
- Celebrate promotions.
- Attend seminars.
- Announce their books.
- Discuss their books on social media.
- Invite them to speak at events.
- Recognize them in the audience when you speak.
- Buy journal ads for their events.

INDUSTRY EVENTS

A professional conference is a rare opportunity not only to deepen your relationships, expand your network, and meet new potential board members but also to enjoy face-to-face time with mentors without the commitment, hassle, and stress of a scheduled meeting. If both you and a board member are attending a professional conference or industry event, such as a National Association of Social Workers annual meeting or the Annual Meeting and Exposition of the American Organization of Nurses or a weekend retreat sponsored by the Trauma Center at Justice Resource Institute, plan at least two to three months in advance to connect with the board member at the event. When you register for the event, reach out to board members to secure time. Make arrangements with key board members for breakfast, lunch, or dinner. Since board members' schedules are likely to be more flexible at industry events, you can have face-to-face time or arrange for an introduction to a sought-after guru. This is the perfect time to have an obligation-free meeting with often overextended and busy board members who are difficult to schedule phone meetings with, let alone in-person consultations. You can also set aside some time, even if only 20 minutes, to have a cup of coffee or tea and catch up with or meet new peers from around the country or around the world with the goal of expanding your network.

ISSUES COMMONLY REQUIRING CONSULTATION WITH BOARD MEMBERS

There are certain issues that every professional will deal with at some point in his or her career for which consulting a Personal Board will give one a definite advantage over others who may not have access to such advice and guidance. The following career milestones and issues you will encounter over the course of your career commonly require the assistance of your Personal Board.

LEARNING ABOUT YOUR PROFESSION AND VARIOUS ROLES

Meet with a variety of different people whose professional lives are interesting to you. You are mining for information about the profession. Finding the right board members is crucial and requires time, tenacity, and the willingness to risk rejection. When you don't know what your goals are, meet with interesting people and talk to them about what they are doing. It would be helpful if they are doing things that are somewhat interesting to you. Reflecting on these conversations helps you to gain a deeper understanding of the role and the profession so you can make an informed decision about your career. Did speaking to this person make you bored, or did what he or she had to say get you excited?

JOB INTERVIEWS

When you are preparing for an important job interview, a mentor can be an invaluable resource in a practical sense and also emotionally. A mentor can conduct a mock interview by asking you the types of questions you may encounter, enabling you to think about and prepare thought-out responses *before* you go into the interview. A mentor can also provide the emotional support and calm you down if you are extremely nervous prior to an interview. Another benefit of consulting board members when preparing for an important job interview is that they can be a source of encouragement and serve to boost your confidence and self-assurance so that you may make the best possible impression at your interview.

FINDING A NEW JOB

Leverage the network of your Personal Board to find openings and positions that are suited to your goals and skills. Your closest mentors, such as the Chairperson of your Board, will be intimately aware of your needs. Sending résumés in cold after rolling job listings has become the least successful way to land a job in today's marketplace, so it is up to you to employ alternative means of discovering open positions in your field. Board members can be an invaluable resource during a job search, not only by informing you of open positions that are suited to your skills and goals but also by introducing you to the decision maker and perhaps even landing you an interview. A sponsor or Chairperson who has a personal stake in your success may actively be on the lookout for specific types of positions that he or she knows you are pursuing or for which he or she thinks you would be well suited. Your board members can help you stand out from the crowd when applying for competitive positions by personally introducing you to the human resources department at an organization with which they are affiliated or giving your résumé to the decision maker outside the usual channels. In this way, you will already have a leg up over other candidates and have a better chance of landing a job. In addition, you will save time and effort by networking through your board to find a job; searching website listings and submitting résumés online can be time- and labor-intensive. Leveraging the contacts on your Personal Board is a tried-and-true method for conducting a successful job search, historically speaking and in our contemporary job market.

Before you start an endeavor, you should evaluate your board's feedback about your innate strengths and talents. If you were looking for a job, you would identify individuals who were connected to your ideal job and possibly appoint them to your Personal Board and suggest a meeting.

Before looking for a job, determine your goals. You should be networking, identifying potential board members, and exploring different aspects of all your possible professional goals. Everyone you meet could potentially be a source of new information that will help you identify a direction in your career and help define your interests and strategically set forth future goals. You are getting more information to make decisions about your next steps.

REFERENCES AND REFERRALS

Everyone always needs references for a potential job. Ask for references from someone who would be most helpful because of their position or their influence. If you have more than one potential reference, focus first on contacts who work at your place of employment, such as your supervisor or boss. Only turn to your board members if they work at the same organization. Board members who do not work at your place of employment are more helpful as referrals. They will be able to make connections with people they may know whether they work within your organization or not.

MAJOR LIFE DECISIONS (THINGS THAT YOU INITIATE)

- Having a baby.
- Getting married.
- Making a major move.
- Taking a risky new job.
- Retiring/rewiring.
- Deciding to divorce.

MAJOR LIFE EVENTS (THINGS THAT HAPPEN TO YOU)

- Getting downsized or laid off.
- Getting fired for cause.
- Recovering from a major professional mistake.
- Having health issues.
- Dealing with family emergencies or family issues.
- Facing financial catastrophe.
- Dealing with public scandal or embarrassment.

MENTORING STYLES

Board members exhibit different mentoring styles, which are often a function of personality type. While the categorization of your board members in terms of the functional area they occupy—whether the technological arena, the legal field, or the sphere of marketing and branding—each of your board members will exhibit a personal mentoring style that can be useful to consider when determining whom to seek out on a particular issue. For example, when you are feeling down and out about not being awarded a promotion, it may be best to turn to the "Cheerleader" or the "Shoulder to Cry On" type of mentor rather than the "Town Crier."

This is a lateral way to consider which mentor to choose for any specific issue with which you need advice or help. First, each mentor is categorized according to his or her function by being assigned to a specific office of your VPBOD. Second, a mentor's string position in each office is fluid and determined on a case-by-case basis; the first string for one case requiring a CFO is not necessarily the best CFO in your roster but may be the best CFO to handle that particular issue. Considering each board member according to his or her mentoring style, as described below, is another way to sort through the growing number of mentors on your Personal Board. It is especially useful to think about a board member's style when one or more mentors are capable of assisting with a particular issue. Although there are certain issues that require input from multiple board members that you will synthesize to determine your course of action, there are others for which you may benefit from having a personal or emotional connection with your mentor.

Each mentor's style may not neatly fall into one of the categories below. Many will demonstrate one or more of the styles outlined below. However, most likely, your board members will have dominant characteristics that qualify them as the "Shoulder to Cry On" type or the "Cheerleader" type. Assigning each board member a style in your board journal or contact directory is not necessary; rather, it is simply a guideline for how to think about your relationship with each mentor and the best way to approach and interact with board members. By analyzing your board members' personalities and learning their particular styles of mentorship, you will benefit from yet another way to choose the proper individuals to whom to turn when you need them.

THE SHOULDER TO CRY ON

Personality: Loyal, emotional, and sensitive.
Function: Providing psychosocial and emotional support in times of need.

The "Shoulder to Cry On" mentoring style is very personalized, emotionally open, and comfortable for both mentor and protégé. You can identify these mentors by their open and nonjudgmental attitude and the ease with which you find yourself opening up to them. You never feel nervous or self-conscious around Shoulder to Cry On mentors; in fact, their goal is getting you to open up to them and reveal your true self so that they can provide the best guidance possible. They are very perceptive and seem to be able to anticipate your reactions to their advice or your choices about important decisions. When you are feeling down and out, feeling insecure, or having a hard time, these types of mentors are excellent resources for emotional support. Although they do indeed have another area of expertise—any one of your board members can be a Shoulder to Cry On type—you may find yourself turning to them for issues outside their specialties simply because you develop a strong connection and bond. In times of stress, trouble, and difficulty, the Shoulder to Cry On type is an invaluable mentor to have on your VPBOD. You trust these mentors and are confident that you can confide in and be honest with them, which enables them to provide you not only with emotional support but also with guidance informed by the totality of a situation rather than the version you edit for public consumption. Usually, the mentors who become Shoulders to Cry On are kindred spirits with whom you share more than just a professional relationship, and your relationship most likely will develop into a stronger bond.

THE HOW-TO MENTOR

Personality: Detail-oriented, thorough, and knowledgeable.
Function: Providing practical support and teaching new things.

When you don't know how to do something specific, you can turn to a mentor with a how-to style for assistance and advice. However, what is most valuable about "How-To Mentors" is their ability to teach others what they know. Your How-To Mentors want to make sure you are able to do whatever it is you are turning to them for help about.

THE CHEERLEADER

Personality: Optimistic, enthusiastic, and energetic.
Function: Giving encouragement and boosting self-esteem.

The "Cheerleader" mentoring style is also quite important to mentees, especially those who may be at a low point emotionally or who have recently suffered a professional blow, such as losing a job or not getting an expected promotion. Mentors who exhibit the Cheerleader style are usually enthusiastic, optimistic, and energetic personalities who are able to instill the same qualities in their mentees. They stand on the sidelines of your career and provide consistent support.

THE FIXER

Personality: Efficient and effective at addressing urgent issues.
Function: Crisis management, dealing with Mistakes.

You know that person you always call whenever there's a crisis or a problem that you don't know how to handle, emergencies such as not being able to start your car or being locked out of your house? Well, this type of mentor, the "Fixer," is *that* person you call when it comes to professional issues. For example, if you are bullied by a coworker, locked in a struggle with your boss, or made a costly error—this person can help you rectify the situation.

THE TOWN CRIER

Personality: Popular, vivacious, and talkative.
Function: Getting the word out, promoting people and events.

You can profit from having a town crier on your board, someone who is enthusiastic about promoting you and your events. They are likely to have a strong network and will take pleasure in sharing information.

Personality: Knows everyone who's anyone, loves meeting new people.
Function: Making introductions and bringing people together.

This person is a fierce networker who is committed to connecting people and is often seen as the go-to person. They tend to be exceptionally helpful with getting the word out and promoting people and events. These mentors are invaluable when you need that elusive connection or introduction.

LEVERAGING YOUR PERSONAL BOARD'S ROSTER

The roster system for the VPBOD has many uses in enabling you to most effectively leverage the mentors of each office on your board. Remember, a fully and well-developed board is characterized by having a variety of mentors occupying each board position. For example, the CFO office may be held by five different individuals whom you consult for financial advice. The roster system comes into play in order to prioritize and categorize the manner in which you engage each of your CFOs. There is a first-string, a second-string, and a third-string position; there is no limit to the number of individuals who can occupy the CFO roster.

The first-string CFO is the mentor you would prefer to utilize for a specific financial issue you need help with because he or she is the best CFO to handle that issue. This mentor will be on your first string when it comes to that issue but may play second or third string when dealing with another issue. A certain person being considered on the first string—which simply means he or she is the go-to person for that area—does not imply that he or she is superior to those on the second, third, or later strings overall. The fluidity of the board structure enables you to constantly shift various mentors into different string positions depending on different variables.

The most important variable to consider when choosing the string positions on a roster is who is the best mentor to handle that issue. You would then, in your head, line up the second person to go to, the third person to go to, and so on. This is also helpful because the first-string, or first-choice, mentor may not be available to help you at that time. So you need a backup. The second and later strings are your backups when it comes to financial issues.

One reason it is important to maintain a roster of mentors for any particular board position is so that you are able to maximize the range of specialties in that particular field by diversifying the individual expertise of each person on the roster and have access to a variety of sources of information. For example, your CFO roster may contain one person who is an expert on taxes, another who is knowledgeable about billing practices, and another who specializes in retirement planning. At different times during your career, you are going to require advice about any one of these specific aspects of your finances. While your first-string CFO may have an overall knowledge of financial issues, he or she may not have any experience with estate planning, or tax write-offs, or any other number of issues. Therefore, you can turn to your second, third, or fourth string for specialized advice on a specific issue.

Another reason to maintain a roster of mentors in any given board category is in order to have the ability to synthesize a number of different opinions when your issue is one that does not have a definitive answer but rather is a decision you must make on your own by weighing various options and evaluating a variety of information. Not every issue that requires the guidance of a mentor can be resolved by simply turning to one advisor; many dilemmas you face will require that you make an educated and informed decision on your own. The more information you have on which to base your decision, the better choices you will be able to make, and having access to a range of opinions from a group of people all specializing in that particular area is essential in amassing as much information as possible for consideration in making an informed assessment about any number of professional decisions.

Maintaining a roster of mentors is useful in general so that you do not rely too heavily on a specific individual when it comes to getting advice about any particular subject. In other words, when you have an issue that any one of the mentors on your CFO roster is able to answer, you can alternate whom you turn to in order to ensure that you aren't taking up too much of one mentor's valuable time. This also ensures that there is someone there when you have an emergency issue that requires the immediate attention of a mentor. Your first-string mentor may not be available, but if you have a roster of other advisors in that same category, you will still have options when it comes to seeking the advice you require in a time-sensitive situation.

Finally, by crafting a board in which each office involves a roster of mentors, you are able to diversify the makeup of the individuals who make up that roster in terms of demographics. In other words, you can ensure that you have access to the advice and perspectives of mentors of various ages, races, genders, and sexual orientations. This is particularly useful when dealing with political issues and with matters related to cultural, age, gender, or racial bias. In addition, you should staff each board office with mentors at different career stages, from entry-level novice to executive, in order to have access to that range of perspectives. Having a well-rounded roster of board members from various demographic groups enables you to be politically sensitive and to see various issues, such as micro-messages, through the eyes of individuals from different demographic groups.

THE STRING SYSTEM

- First string does not imply that this person is the best mentor on the roster for an office.
- First string is your first choice for a particular issue.
- Second and later strings are your backups if your first string is unavailable, in the order in which you would approach each individual.

THE DIFFERENCE BETWEEN A MENTOR AND A SPONSOR

Another way you may leverage the power of your Personal Board is by forging a strong relationship with a sponsor. Many times the goal for a relationship with a mentor is for that relationship to evolve into a sponsorship. The more sponsors you have, the better; you can never have too many sponsors. A sponsor is so much more than just a mentor. Remember that you need both mentors and sponsors on your board. The two are not the same. Mentors give you career strategies and day-to-day advice. Sponsors open doors and vouch for you. Developing multiple sponsors is crucial to achieving your highest goals. Nurturing relationships with leaders who share your values, have connections and expertise, and may become sponsors is a career-long process. Strong sponsors must have many resources and extensive influence; they are not only advocates for you, but they also offer connections to help you achieve your goals. A sponsor can help propel your career to the next level and beyond. Your success also greatly affects the influence and status of the sponsor. The alliance is indeed a win-win when it is working well. It is never too early for you to act as sponsor for younger mentees, in fact; it will help you to expand your influence and develop your leadership skills. A sponsor adds legitimacy to you and your work and puts his or her reputation to work for you. A sponsor must feel very comfortable with you and have trust in you; after all, the sponsor's name and reputation are on the line. If your sponsor recommends you for a position and you fail to perform, this will reflect badly on him or her. Therefore, the relationship with your sponsor is built on trust more than anything. Your loyalty and making your sponsors shine is a consistent part of the contract in order to nurture the relationship.

Mentors offer psychosocial support for personal and professional development, career advice, and coaching, according to Kathy Kram. Only sponsors actively advocate for advancement. "Classic mentoring" (ideal but rare) combines psychosocial and career support. Workers often get one or the other. If they get both, it's often from different sources.

WHAT YOU CAN DO FOR BOARD MEMBERS

> To build a network, always think of how you can help other people in your network. People like to help people who help them.
>
> Jerry Bruckner

Your board members perform certain tasks that have value to you and your career. In turn, it is important that you make an effort to return the favor by contributing something of value to your board members. This is not only to repay them for their service to you but also is a way you can learn new things, witness your mentors in their element, and pick up on important qualities you may emulate. If you represent a valuable resource in their professional, or even personal, lives, your board members will be more motivated to help you in your endeavors.

Examples of how a mentee can be a valuable resource include a mentor asking you to consider one of his or her other mentees for a position, to meet with a colleague to discuss some details about your area of expertise, or to connect him or her with someone on your staff. Other examples of how a mentee can contribute to mentors or board members:

- Giving feedback on an organization that a mentor is considering consulting.
- Making recommendations for an open position at the mentor's organization.
- Fulfilling a mentor's request for information about the salary range for workers at the mentee's institution.
- Referring colleagues to mentors for job openings in their organizations.
- Assisting with research or other time-limited tasks that a mentor may not have time for.
- Doing a research project for a board member.
- Going to a conference or a speech that a board member is giving.
- Helping with a PowerPoint presentation, especially if the mentor has limited technology skills.
- Where appropriate, referring people to a mentor's services.
- Recommending a mentor for speaking or consulting assignments.
- Singing mentors' praises publicly whether they are present or not.
- Using the wisdom gained from a mentor to pay it forward.
- Being responsive to any request a mentor makes on behalf of others.

FAMOUS MENTORING PAIRS: SPORTS AND ATHLETICS

Mentor	Mentee
Hank Aaron, US baseball player	Dusty Baker, US baseball coach
Bob Bowman, US Olympic swimming coach	Michael Phelps, US swimmer and Olympic gold medalist
Waldemar de Brito, Brazilian footballer	Pelé, Brazilian footballer
Cris Carter, US football Hall of Fame player	Randy Moss, US football player
Angelo Dundee, US boxing trainer	Muhammad Ali, US boxer
Butch Harmon, US golf instructor	Tiger Woods, US golfer
Phil Jackson, US basketball coach	Michael Jordan, US basketball player
Jackie Joyner-Kersee, US track and field athlete and Olympic gold medalist	Dawn Harper, US track and field athlete and Olympic gold medalist
Hamaas Abdul Khaalis, Hanafi Muslim leaderBruce Lee, Hong Kong-US martial artist and actor	Kareem Abdul-Jabbar, US basketball playerJackie Chan, Hong Kong martial artist and actor
Rocky Marciano, US boxer	Ingemar Johansson, US boxing trainer
Eddy Merckx, Belgian cyclist	Lance Armstrong, US cyclist
Joe Montana, US football player	Steve Young, US football player
Antonio Palafox, Mexican tennis player	John McEnroe, US tennis player
Charles Riley, US Olympic track and field coach	Jesse Owens, US track and field athlete and Olympic gold medalist
Matthias Ruth, Babe Ruth's brother	Babe Ruth, US baseball player
Pam Shriver, US tennis player	Venus Williams, US tennis player
Bill Walsh, US football coach	Joe Montana, US football player

PROFILES IN MENTORSHIP: MICHAEL JACKSON AND KOBE BRYANT

The mentoring relationship between star L.A. Lakers basketball star Kobe Bryant (figure 7.2) and musical superstar Michael Jackson (figure 7.3) illustrates many different mentoring principles. First of all, it demonstrates cross-industry mentorship and reiterates the fact that a mentor does not have to belong to the same profession or field as the mentee. Second, it demonstrates the principles of invisible mentorship, in that Bryant looked to Jackson as a role model and a source of inspiration before he knew him personally.

FIGURE 7.2 Mentee: Kobe Bryant, NBA basketball player.

"It sounds weird, I guess, but it's true: I was really mentored by the preparation of Michael Jackson.... We would always talk about how he prepared to make his music, how he prepared for concerts," Bryant said. "He would teach me what he did: how to make a 'Thriller' album, a 'Bad' album, all the details that went into it. It was all the validation that I needed—to know that I had to focus on my craft and never waver. Because what he did—and how he did it—was psychotic. He helped me get to a level where I was able to win three titles playing with Shaq because of my preparation, my study. And it's only all grown. That's the mentality that I have—it's not an athletic one. It's not from [Michael] Jordan. It's not from

FIGURE 7.3 Mentor: Michael Jackson, singer, songwriter, dancer, philanthropist.

other athletes. It's from Michael Jackson" (http://sports.yahoo.com/news/kobe-s till-tough-assists-greats-133500519--nba.html).

"One of the things he always told me was, don't be afraid to be different. In other words, when you have that desire, that drive, people are going to try to pull you away from that, and pull you closer to the pack to be 'normal.' And he was saying, It's OK to be that driven; it's OK to be obsessed with what you want to do. That's perfectly fine. Don't be afraid to not deviate from that. One of the books that he gave me that helped him communicate with me was *Jonathan Livingston Seagull*, which was about that" (http://content. time.com/time/specials/packages/article/0,28804,1907409_1907413_1907488,00. html#ixzz2ptHtVOBp).

"Beyond the genius of what he was, he was just a genuinely, genuinely nice person," Bryant wrote of Jackson. "He was just a genuinely nice person who was exceptionally bright, exceptionally bright, and driven and talented. You mix those things together, man, you have Michael Jackson" (http://www.huffingtonpost. com/2010/11/23/kobe-bryant-michael-jacks_n_787780.html).

"Michael was extremely misunderstood. He was just so generous, extremely giving and caring. Aside from us talking about work and how each other prepare and train for things, he introduced me to things I would never ever watch. *American in Paris. Breakfast at Tiffany's.* I would never watch those movies. You know what I mean? He introduced those to me, opened my eyes to a whole 'nother side to things. Appreciate Fred Astaire's talent, things like that, kinda seeing how that relates to basketball. We used to have those kinds of conversations all the time. He's just such a giver and just a beautiful person" (http://www.youtube. com/watch?v=xMgDhIJjWpc).

KNOWLEDGE NUGGETS

- It is important to maintain a roster of mentors for any particular board position so that you are able to maximize the range of specialties in that particular field.
- Subcommittees are especially useful for addressing short-term issues that occur during the course of your day-to-day work life. They are also helpful when you need a quick turnaround on a pressing question or issue.
- Remember that you need both mentors and sponsors on your board. Mentors give you career strategies and day-to-day advice, while sponsors open doors and vouch for you.
- Each of your board members will exhibit a personal mentoring style that can be useful to consider when determining whom to seek out on a particular issue.
- By analyzing your board members' personalities and learning their particular styles of mentorship, you will benefit from yet another way to choose the proper individuals to turn to when you need them.

CHAPTER 8

MAINTAINING YOUR VIRTUAL BOARD

You have to water the flowers you want to grow.

Stephen Covey

Once you have set your goals, made your connections, appointed mentors to your Virtual Personal Board of Directors, and begun regularly leveraging its resources, your job is by no means done. To continue the smooth functioning of your Personal Board and ensure that it is maximally effective in helping you develop and grow your career, you must continually maintain it.

Building a VPBOD is like cultivating a garden. You must first prepare and till the soil, which corresponds to the initial self-reflection and goal-setting process. Once the field is ready to be sown, you may then begin to plant seeds, which relates to the preliminary stage of making new connections and meeting with potential mentors. As the seeds you have sown sprout and grow into seedlings (acquaintances) and eventually plants (contacts), you can then evaluate and choose those that you would most like to nurture, just as you appoint certain mentors to specific board positions and decide to develop particular relationships over others. Once you have a field of maturing plants competing for light and water, where one plant requires full sun while others prefer shade, you, the gardener, must arrange and rearrange them according to your needs and preferences. This part of the process is very much like what you will eventually need to do for you board: carefully select your mentors' positions on your Personal Board according their individual strengths and the particular requirements of your career goals at each point of your professional development.

Ultimately, after investing a great deal of time and energy in its cultivation and development, you will achieve perfection. Every plant will be situated in its ideal location, where it regularly receives the proper amount of light and water, and will therefore produce healthy, beautiful, and plentiful blooms, with which you may assemble elegant and magnificent floral bouquets. Similarly, your Personal Board will also reach a point of productivity: every office will be occupied by ideal mentors, possessing wide-ranging information and a diversity of perspectives, providing you with an extensive selection of flowers of wisdom to harvest when the time comes.

However, anyone who has ever gardened knows that a gardener's job is never really done. Even when your garden seems to have reached the point of perfection, there are always weeds to be pulled, plants to be pruned, fertilizer to be applied, and mulch to be laid. Likewise, your Personal Board is never "perfect" or "complete." Just as a flower garden requires constant maintenance and nurturing in order to flourish and produce the most fragrant and beautiful blooms, so does your Personal Board.

ACHIEVING VPBOD EXPERTISE

After you have established your Personal Board and have begun leveraging its resources on a regular basis, your ultimate goal is to integrate it seamlessly into your professional routine. At that point, you will have achieved a level of expertise that will increase your confidence and enable you to further your career each and every time you engage a mentor for assistance, advice, or connections. This level of proficiency is akin to having the wagon wheel representing your board perfectly functioning; you and your board are rolling smoothly on the road to your ultimate vision for your professional future and to the realization of your best self.

The length of time that is required to reach this pivotal point of seamless integration and total proficiency at leveraging a Personal Board into one's professional repertoire is different for everyone. Certain individuals may achieve expert VPBOD capability after just one year; others may take up to three years to establish a fully formed and functioning developmental network. There are many contributing factors that determine a person's ability to get from the starting point to the finish line—from the patch of dusty, uncultivated dirt to the lush and flourishing garden. The three factors that most significantly influence the length of time it takes to develop expertise in leveraging a fully functional Personal Board are:

1. Your level of commitment and motivation.
2. Your personality and innate character traits.
3. Your specific profession and its defining qualities.

Each of these determining factors can represent either an asset or a challenge.

LEVEL OF COMMITMENT AND MOTIVATION

A person who is organized, ambitious, and motivated to establish his or her developmental network will gain proficiency and expertise in the VPBOD methodology more quickly than an unenthusiastic individual who only halfheartedly pursues the development of a Personal Board. Having a VPBOD at your disposal may make professional advancement easy, but gathering the contacts, building your network, and finally putting it to work for you is *not*. Achieving expertise in building and leveraging the resources of a VPBOD takes patience, persistence, and dedication. Therefore, the length of time it takes to build a fully functional VPBOD is very much dependent on your level of commitment and determination to enhance your professional development using a Personal Board.

A high level of *enthusiasm* is a major asset when it comes to building and maintaining a Personal Board, especially at the outset of the process. It is easy to get disheartened after feeling rejected by a potential mentor or discouraged when a specific individual in whom you are interested does not respond when you reach out. This is why *commitment* to your VPBOD is so important. Despite any discouragement you need to overcome along the way, once you are rolling with your Personal Board and begin experiencing the enormous professional advantages it affords, your *motivation* will skyrocket. Each and every time you enjoy the benefits of your VPBOD, your incentive to continue building and perfecting it will increase. The more you leverage the assets of your Personal Board, the more they will pay off for you. At a certain crucial point, working with your Personal Board will become second nature. Rather than treating it as something separate from your career development, your VPBOD will become *integral* and *fundamental* to your professional advancement.

Being highly organized is a personality trait that will enhance your ability to quickly achieve expertise working with a VPBOD. A well-developed Personal Board will consist of numerous current, past, and potential mentors; general professional contacts; current and past coworkers; and, after a certain developmental threshold, current and potential mentees. Because of the sheer magnitude of connections, maintaining a well-developed VPBOD entails utilizing a streamlined, easily referenced, and comprehensive contact database. It is essential to successful and effective management. An example is the "Mentor Contact Directory" app in the online VPBOD system.

PERSONALITY AND CHARACTER TRAITS

Your particular personality traits are an important factor in determining how quickly and easily you will be able to achieve proficiency in leveraging your VPBOD. Some people may not have difficulty making the connections and maintaining the relationships that are the most essential and primary aspects of the Personal Board. However, someone who is more of an introvert, or perhaps even painfully shy or experiencing social phobia, may need to tailor his or her networking plan to having more one-on-one interactions. The key is to be clear about your personality type and the challenges that it presents. With proper planning and support, a VPBOD is quite possible. It is important to acknowledge your personal challenges and seek a board member's help with strategies to work around them. Toastmasters International is an excellent resource if you are shy or have difficulty with networking. Additionally, social media may be a helpful part of your strategic plan.

Author and introversion expert Susan Cain defines shyness as "the fear of negative judgment." Introversion, on the other hand, is "a preference for quiet, minimally stimulating environments" (Susan Cain's blog, http://www.thepowerofintroverts.com/).

In either case, creating and maintaining a VPBOD can be a special challenge but is not unachievable. Since the core of networking is socialization, Cain, author of *QUIET: The Power of Introverts in a World That Can't Stop Talking*, 2013, recommends a "socialization quota" for introverts. You can decide on the number of social events that you will attend over a period of time, for example, committing to one per week or four per month. This helps to lessen the struggle and guilt associated with the commitment of attending networking events. (Patkar, 2013, http://lifehacker.com/network-better-as-an-introvert-with-a-socialization-qu-1465458942) Another great resource for introverts is *Self-Promotion for Introverts: The Quiet Guide to Getting Ahead*, by Nancy Ancowitz, 2009. It offers many insights and tips that can be helpful in building your board.

SOCIAL PHOBIA (SOCIAL ANXIETY DISORDER)

Most people are often somewhat shy or self-conscious on occasions such as when meeting or interacting with famous or powerful people or giving speeches. However, social phobias can cause tremendous anxiety that could prevent some individuals from performing these tasks at all.

According to the National Institute of Mental Health, social phobia is a strong fear of being judged by others and of being embarrassed. This fear can be so strong that it gets in the way of going to work or school or doing other everyday things.

Some of the triggers for social phobia are:

- Meeting new people.
- Making small talk.
- Speaking to or connecting with "important" people.
- Interactions with authority figures.
- Making phone calls.
- Attending social events.
- Eating or drinking in public.
- Speaking up in a meeting.

Social phobias can be truly paralyzing. For example, one of my coaching clients, a successful senior corporate compliance officer, would worry and lose sleep for weeks before she was to attend her company's quarterly board meeting. She would get a migraine headache days before the meeting. She would call in sick to avoid these experiences. (Other common symptoms are racing heartbeats, a tightness in the chest, feeling faint, sweating, and nausea.)

Another one of my clients, a very brilliant and skilled corporate attorney, would begin to shake uncontrollably before his biweekly staff meetings with his senior partners and colleagues. At the meetings, he would usually lose his voice and would often freeze in mid-sentence when he did have to speak.

These situations were incredibly distressing to both individuals, in addition to being potential career killers.

Many sufferers handle social phobia by:

- Avoiding social situations, especially networking.
- Shunning the spotlight, remaining silent, or hiding in the background.
- Requiring company for every outing.
- Self-medicating with drinks or drugs.

All of these things present a challenge to building a VPBOD.

Social phobia can be treated with psychotherapy or medication. Both of my above-mentioned clients received excellent results from a combination of the two and were able to build solid VPBODs.

- Psychotherapy can help a person develop alternative ways of thinking and enhance their social skills.
- Medication, including many antianxiety drugs, is extremely helpful. A good psychiatrist can come up with the right combination to produce amazing results.

If you are struggling with untreated a social phobia, there is no need to suffer in silence; you can get the help you need to make a VPBOD possible at your own rate.

Your unique character traits play a major role in determining not only how long it will take you to find and develop appropriate mentors but also how you will manage and how effectively you will leverage these relationships as resources for career advancement. Maintaining multiple relationships with a large number of professional colleagues is fundamental to cultivating a smoothly, effectively functioning Personal Board.

CHARACTERISTICS OF YOUR PROFESSION

The development of a Personal Board and the accomplishment of VPBOD expertise may progress more slowly or quickly depending on your particular profession or the specific field in which you are employed. A fundraiser or salesperson, for whom meeting people and socializing are a primary job responsibility, will, of course, find networking and making new contacts less difficult than most, and building their boards will present less of a challenge. On the other hand, a scientific researcher who spends most of his or her time in the lab, having contact with few, may have to make a focused effort to "break out" and expand his or her network of contacts.

Every field has its pros and cons when it comes to building and using a Personal Board, as does every profession. Some fields, such as politics and entertainment, lend themselves perfectly to the development of Personal Boards, since networking is fundamental to success in those specific fields. Other professions, such as art and science, are intrinsically the types of endeavors that foster, if not require, solitude. Therefore, many professionals in these fields are not naturally adept at the networking aspects of building and using a Personal Board. Nonetheless, leveraging a VPBOD will always benefit the career of any professional in any field. The degree to which people may advance their careers with a

Personal Board is dependent, however, on their commitment and dedication to overcoming the obstacles in their way and leveraging the assets in their favor.

However long it takes a person to reach the "tipping point" of achieving VPBOD mastery, the most important ongoing task becomes board maintenance. Just as a wagon wheel requires repair from time to time—spokes break and have to be replaced, the outer wheel may splinter and crack, or the axle may need replacement—so, too, does your board. The framework requires constant tweaking and maintenance so that you can continue rolling smoothly on the path to your goals. In this chapter, we review the central principles to remember to keep your VPBOD relevant to where you are in your career and to your goals and aspirations.

Remember that although the Personal Board is based on a definitive structure and using it effectively requires adhering to explicit Rules of Engagement, the body of your VPBOD must always remain fluid and flexible. Just as you are always changing and growing, both personally and professionally, your board must also constantly evolve and develop in order to accommodate your professional needs and desires at any given point in time—in terms of changing goals, career advancement, and personal circumstances.

MAINTAINING YOUR PERSONAL BOARD

As your career evolves and progresses, so will your VPBOD. The mentors you initially assemble for your board at the outset of your career will, of course, be different from those on your board mid-career or toward the end of your career. The board-building process is continual; as you advance professionally, your requirements of your board members will change. You must weed out mentors who no longer serve a purpose, nurture relationships with board members whose assets become more relevant, and add new mentors when no one on your current roster can fulfill the advisory needs of a new aspect of your career.

For example, if you created your Personal Board when you were an entry-level salesperson at a retail clothing store, you may have staffed your board with mentors who possessed knowledge and experience in retail sales and customer service, along with other entry-level salespeople as peer mentors to whom you could turn for sympathetic support and practical guidance. As your career progressed and you became more knowledgeable about the retail clothing field, you might have decided to pursue a career as a buyer. Once you made the decision to go in that direction in your career, you would have to add board members with specific experience as buyers, knowledge of inventory management, and also familiarity with vendor relations. Once you achieved the transition and were officially promoted to the title of buyer, you would have to supplement your board roster with additional mentors who had the knowledge, expertise, and experience to fulfill the advisory and practical mentoring needs required by your new position.

While your Personal Board requires constant maintenance to keep it relevant to your current career position, there are specific situations in which routine board maintenance is not sufficient. One of these situations is when you are considering changing professions, either within your own field or by moving into a completely different field. Another is when you are striving for a major promotion to middle-management or executive positions.

In cases such as these, board maintenance becomes more like tweaking or fine-tuning your board, because both require that you completely reassess not only the makeup of your board but also your specific needs and requirements at that point in time.

FINE-TUNING AND TWEAKING YOUR PERSONAL BOARD

FINE-TUNING FOR A CAREER CHANGE

If you are on a certain career track in a specific profession, the majority of the mentors on your Personal Board will continue to have assets you can leverage for the duration of your career. However, if you are considering transitioning into a completely different field, for example, leaving a position as a teacher at an elementary school to become a Web developer at an interactive agency, your Personal Board is going to require more than just routine maintenance. In this type of situation, your VPBOD needs a major overhaul.

Although you will need to add a number of mentors in many different offices, most of your board members will be able to remain on your board, albeit in a less important role. You will have to staff certain offices, such as that of the Professional Guru, with a totally new roster of mentors appropriate to your new title or profession. However, other offices, such as your Chairperson of the Board or CFO, may remain exactly the same, primarily because their expertise is not title- or profession-specific. Remember, your Chairperson is the mentor with whom you have the most personal relationship, who is privy to more intimate details of your life and can give you informed guidance and advice based on his or her knowledge of you as an individual. Therefore, your Chairperson can usually transition with you in the case of a radical mid-career shift from one industry to another.

Likewise, the office of the CFO is staffed with mentors who advice you regarding all manner of financial issues, and their guidance will still be applicable no matter what field you are working in. However, unlike the Chairperson position, the CFO office may need to be supplemented if you are transitioning to a job where there are finance-specific aspects with which you will require guidance, such as opening your own business or starting your own practice.

FINE-TUNING FOR CAREER ADVANCEMENT

For every move you make in your career, you need to reassess your relationships on the board, because every new move requires that you shift your relationships with board members. For example, when you get a promotion from supervisor to director, you want to make sure that you have enough resources on your board to assist you with the types of issues that an executive will need help with. That is not to say that you eliminate board members who were primarily there to assist you with your middle-management role; you simply reposition them and promote other members to more prominent places on your board.

WHEN TO ADD NEW MENTORS

You are always looking to add new mentors, but there are specific times when you especially need to seek out new board members. You may find them simply by networking with existing board members, but if no board members have contacts in the area you need help with, you may need to look outside your network. Add new board members when:

- You make a radical shift in your career, such as a vertical move (a promotion)—you need more contacts to be peer mentors at your new level.
- You relocate to a new geographic area—you need to expand your network board to include people in your new location.
- Your career gets off track (you get downsized or fired)—you need fresh contacts from a completely different area, new blood, new connections.

OUTGROWING YOUR SPONSORS, CHAIRPERSONS, OR PROFESSIONAL GURUS

Sometimes as you progress in your career, you may find yourself outgrowing some particularly important board positions: sponsors, Chairpersons, and professional gurus. You need something that they can't offer you, so you will demote the current members in prominence on your Personal Board and promote some of the later strings to first string.

ELIMINATING OR REPLACING MEMBERS

A situation may arise where you have to cut ties with a board member, especially if there a public disgrace. You have a need on your board to fulfill through this board member, but he or she is no longer respected in the profession. You may maintain a relationship with this person personally—you don't need to cut ties entirely—but you may have to eliminate him or her as an official member of your Personal Board. This is where the lack of formality comes in handy: because there is no formal arrangement, you do not have to deal with the awkwardness of formally dismissing someone from your board; you simply phase the person out and stop referring to him or her for assistance, contacts, and information, promoting someone else in the category to take his or her place or, if the person's contributions were very unique and you don't have another resource, seeking out a new member to replace the old one.

Just because you don't further your relationship with that particular person, that does not mean that you cut ties with the people he or she introduced you to, as those people may still be useful on your board. However, by the same token, you may want to vet the former member's contacts more deeply after discovering some serious ethical issue, particularly the former member's closest contacts if they are members of your board, in order to avoid further association with people who may pose a threat to your own professional reputation.

Publicly distance yourself from someone whose reputation has been tarnished or who has been exposed for fraud or professionally disgraced. There is usually no need to make public statements or announcements. In these situations, silence is golden. "No comment" is often the best solution. You want to honor the contributions that the board member made to you and your career by not adding to the price that disgrace has cost your board member. There is no virtue in public judging.

EVALUATING BOARD MEMBERS' CHANGING ROLES

At a certain point in time, you may find that board members on whom you once relied for everything are no longer relevant to your current place in your career. You may have surpassed a particular mentor's position. You can show your gratitude by keeping him or her on in an emeritus status. Such mentors are removed from your active-duty roster but retain their titles for recognition for their prior contributions toward advancing your career. You might acknowledge them personally on birthday, holidays, and so on, and invite them to public events where appropriate. Publicly acknowledge them during speeches, in your new book, at openings, during any celebratory event, and so on, as appropriate. How you treat emeritus members is a reflection on you and your character.

YOUR PERSONAL BOARD THROUGHOUT YOUR CAREER

Depending on what stage of your career you are navigating, your Personal Board will play different roles in your professional development. At certain stages, your Personal Board may be crucial to your professional success, particularly during the advancement stage. In other phases, primarily the late phase, your Personal Board will be less important to your own success and more significant for assisting mentees and subordinates.

ESTABLISHMENT CAREER PHASE

During the **establishment career phase**, you are looking for or starting your first job, or you are starting out in a new career. At this stage, you need to learn as much as you can about your field, your profession, and the role of your specific title. One way to do this is by consulting and comparing notes with peer mentors, seeking the guidance of Professional Gurus, and emulating boss-mentors.

ESTABLISHMENT CAREER PHASE ROLES AND TITLES

- Students.
- Recent graduates.
- Entry-level positions.

ESTABLISHMENT CAREER PHASE FUNCTIONS OF A PERSONAL BOARD

- Finding direction.
- Learning about one or more fields.
- Learning about one or more professions.
- Recommendations and references.
- Getting your first job.
- Positive reinforcement and confirmation.
- Member contact directory.

ADVANCEMENT CAREER PHASE

During the **advancement career phase**, you are in passionate pursuit of long-term career objectives. Your position may require that you learn something outside your comfort zone or above your level of expertise, and you have opportunities to proactively learn new skills, take on more responsibilities, and be noticed by higher-ups. During the advancement phase, you may be promoted to a new role in your organization, be awarded a more advanced title at a new organization, or make a lateral move to a new service area or field.

ADVANCEMENT CAREER PHASE ROLES AND TITLES

- Supervisors.
- Middle managers.

ADVANCEMENT CAREER PHASE FUNCTIONS OF A PERSONAL BOARD

- Learning the ropes of the profession.
- Making connections inside the field.
- Getting a second job at a new organization.
- Being promoted to a more advanced title at your own organization.

- Being introduced to peers and colleagues.
- Finding a mentor to sponsor you.
- Gaining knowledge of office politics
- Identifying and emulating role models.

MIDDLE CAREER PHASE

During the **middle career phase**, you are a seasoned professional who is confident in your capabilities. You are comfortable in the position you have achieved, and your primary focus is on accomplishment and recognition from peers, colleagues, and higher-ups. You begin mentoring and developing subordinates as a means to pay it forward, prevent career stagnation, and stay in touch with the rank-and-file of the organization.

MIDDLE CAREER PHASE ROLES AND TITLES

- Managerial positions.
- Executive-level positions.
- Board-level positions.

MIDDLE CAREER PHASE FUNCTIONS OF A PERSONAL BOARD

- Developing subordinates.
- Distinguishing yourself from the crowd.
- Deepening organizational knowledge.
- Changing roles or professions.
- Being mindful about career stagnation.
- Assistance with career revitalization.
- Maintaining strong ties with colleagues.
- Increasing the chances of getting choice assignments.
- Obtaining psychosocial support with organizational change, such as getting downsized, losing your job, or your position being phased out or becoming obsolete.
- Learning how to cultivate mentoring relationships with your own mentees.

LATE CAREER PHASE

You are well established in a management or executive role with authority. Your focus is on preserving and perpetuating the work you have accomplished over the course of your career. Colleagues, co-workers, and subordinates look up to you as an expert or repository of professional know-how in your field. You are commended for your professional achievements with awards, board positions, and other honors.

LATE CAREER PHASE ROLES OR TITLES

- Departmental director.
- Vice president, senior vice president, or other executive.
- Retiring (rewiring).
- Postretirement activities.

LATE CAREER PHASE FUNCTIONS OF A PERSONAL BOARD

- Increasing visibility in your profession.
- Providing a role model to subordinates and younger board members.
- Developing subordinates and mentees.
- Identifying advancement opportunities for mentees.
- Passing on wisdom and knowledge to newcomers to the profession.
- Collaborating with colleagues to promote or encourage organizational growth.
- Providing organizational leadership and guiding the development of the profession.
- Review of and rewards for past accomplishments.
- Staying connected to organizations.
- Staying connected to younger generations.
- Acclimating the next generation of the profession.
- Fortifying your legacy.

ORGANIZING YOUR VPBOD WITH A BOARD MEMBER DIRECTORY

As your board grows and evolves, keep updating a well-organized directory of board members in an electronic contact database, such as the VPBOD system online at www.VirtualPersonalBoard.com. Here are some tips:

- Customize a contact program such as Microsoft Outlook or Apple Address Book to create a board member directory.
- Use a Microsoft Excel spreadsheet with a column for each field to maintain your directory.

- Create a Google Contact Database and customize it according to the information categories listed in the directory entry.
- Create a Google Circle, Facebook group, or LinkedIn group to assemble all your board members on a social media platform.

BOARD MEMBER DIRECTORY ENTRY

Vital Stats

Name:

Title:

Address:

Mobile number:

Personal e-mail:

Birthday:

Special information (hobbies, pets, etc.):

Professional Information

Company:

Company address:

Job title:

Work number:

Work e-mail:

LinkedIn profile:

Facebook profile:

Professional website:

Blog site(s):

Publication URLs:

Book(s) published:

VPBOD-Specific Information

Board office:

Board office appointment date:

String position:

Mentor type (situational, boss, peer, etc.):

Rating (bronze, silver, gold)

Introduced by:

First met place and date:

References by (people your board member has referred you to):

References to (people you have referred to your board member):

First meeting date, place, notes:

Documenting Meetings

(Subsequent meetings organized by date)

Date of next meeting: Document details

CULTIVATING YOURSELF WITH A PERSONAL EDUCATION PLAN

Learning is a treasure that will follow its owner everywhere.

Chinese proverb

A central part of maintaining your board is keeping your educational agenda up to date. Your Personal Education Plan (PEP) should be suited to your needs at any point in your career. The objective of maintaining a PEP is to solidify your career aspirations. The first way to achieve this goal is to locate and listen for your passions by expanding your horizons and broadening your perspectives through your PEP activities. The second way is to learn as much as you can about your field by pursuing activities that broaden your perspectives about it, such as:

- Join a LinkedIn group.
- Follow the blogs of superstars in your field.
- Watch TED Talks on YouTube.
- Participate in webinars.

Your Education Officers can help guide you to the proper educational pursuits for your particular goals and ambitions, and they will be an important resource for information and advice about furthering your education. Having more than one Education Officer, with different skill sets, is important. They will give you their take on the profession and give you hints and contacts about how you can improve your educational profile. You should also be reading books, attending workshops, and researching online to supplement your knowledge of your field. To begin designing your PEP, first consider where you are in your career right now.

CASE STUDIES 1: PEP AFTER A PROMOTION

Joanne just got a promotion to a directorship. She went to a meeting with another director, and what she learned was that strategic planning was the most important part of the job. After this meeting, she enrolled in a college course on strategic planning.

In a meeting with a board member who was a seasoned director, Lola realized that as a new community educator, being able to create PowerPoint presentations would be helpful in communicating with the community. She then enrolled in two-week computer workshop to learn how to use PowerPoint and prepare presentations.

Sue enrolled in a three-session training course on progressive discipline to help in her new supervisory role. The goal was to be able to feel especially competent in her new role and therefore feel more confident.

THRIVING BUT STILL STRIVING

You are in a position and doing a good job, and you enjoy what you are doing. You receive positive feedback from your boss and coworkers and are connecting well with colleagues. You want to take advantage of all this by increasing your influence and becoming the go-to person to raise your profile. Your goal: to expand your professional reach. For example, say you are in the research department and are content with your job. An announcement arrives that the institution is looking for someone to be on its organization-wide taskforce to cut down on turnover. It does not have anything to do with your current job, but because your goal is to expand your influence, you volunteer to be the representative from your division. The goal is to be seen as a leader, to be known by more people, to get experience and exposure in something that you are not particularly knowledgeable about, to get to know the organization better, and to meet people you don't know. In choosing these kinds of assignments, you should first question how they could be helpful to you. You might want to consult with your Education Officer to discuss the value of volunteer assignments. Create a strategy for each one as it comes along to assess its value to you. Your educational plan is not only about learning in a classroom setting, but it is also about taking advantage of opportunities that come along that enable you to learn more about your profession.

IMPROVING NEGATIVE WORK CONDITIONS

Do any of the following apply to you?

- You are reacting to a negative evaluation.
- There is excessive turnover in your organization.

- You were denied or passed over for a promotion.
- You are experiencing conflict with your boss or coworkers.
- You are experiencing dissatisfaction in your role, and you are questioning if this is the right direction for you.
- You feel stuck in a rut, and your passion for the role is waning; you may be experiencing burnout.
- You are not doing well with your boss; your boss is unappreciative of or uninterested in you, and you do not connect with your coworkers.

If you were passed over for a promotion, go to a board member and acknowledge that you are feeling angry or hurt; you want to have an objective ear to listen to your situation so you can get somebody else's take on it. Your mentor will share what might be the reason you were passed over and will help you come up with an action plan to work on that aspect of yourself. Perhaps you were a strong contender but someone else had more experience as a leader, or maybe you weren't holding your team accountable. You are going to hear all the feedback, and during that consultation, it might become clear that you need some added education in one or more areas. You can then think about how to address your challenges. For example, if you have had trouble managing difficult employees, you can take advantage of an HR program on holding employees accountable or having difficult dialogue. You must know the difference between being liked and being respected. Instead of getting mad and leaving, take it as an opportunity to learn something new and improve your skill set.

LOOKING TO MOVE AHEAD

Perhaps one of the following applies to you:

- You want a promotion or a new job.
- You want to leave your position for a new one.
- Your boss is leaving, and you are a junior on staff, but you want his job.
- There is a new division opening up; you don't have the required education, but you have corporate experience.

For example, your organization offers service to seniors, infants, and mothers. You would like to be the VP of the organization, and you have only worked in one division. Your goal: to assess your career history for transferable skills. The idea would be talk to board members and employees who are in parts of the organization that you don't know about and take a course on leadership. At the same time, do regular reading about aspects of the service that you don't know about.

Depending on which phase you are at in your career, you should be pursuing a customized educational plan specifically tailored to your needs and ambitions.

ADVANCEMENT EDUCATIONAL PLAN

If you are at the establishment or advancement phase of your career, you should pursue an advancement educational plan. Analyzing what is happening in the overall profession and researching aspects of the industry will help you sharpen your professional vision. Make a list of the people you need to meet and why. Remember, education isn't just about taking a class—your Personal Board is a major educational resource. If you are establishing yourself or actively pursuing career advancement, you can also increase your knowledge and pursue education by:

- Meeting with members of your board and mining them for information.
- Participating in online workshops.
- Following blogs and social media related to the area.
- Taking a college course.
- Reading and exploration—staying on top of what's going on in the industry.
- Subscribing to industry publications.
- Joining a professional organization and attending conferences.
- Joining online groups on LinkedIn or other peer groups.
- Maintaining a professional blog.
- Giving presentations at industry conferences.
- Looking for opportunities to collaborate with colleagues.
- Updating your résumé.

MAINTENANCE EDUCATIONAL PLAN

- Think about how better to do the job that you have.
- You always have to be ready to move ahead. Look at how you might get better in your current position.
- How might you hone your skills or become an expert in your current position?
- Build your network, become the go-to person, build your influence, solidify your visibility, solidify your relationships, and build your support system.

CULTIVATING YOURSELF WITH YOUR PERSONAL WELLNESS PLAN

A wise man ought to realize that health is his most valued possession.

Hippocrates

Your health is your wealth. Maintaining your Personal Board becomes just another aspect of maintaining yourself—and your health—once you have fully and seamlessly integrated your

VPBOD into the functioning of your life. In order to perform at the highest level profession-ally, you must make it a priority to take care of yourself physically, spiritually, and mentally. It's important to have an active role in pursuing events and activities to keep you healthy.

Keeping a daily journal, reading meditation books or other favorite books, and mental health days where you go to a day spa or catching up with an old friend for a whole after-noon are great ways to keep you mentally healthy. If you have a conference coming up, consider clearing your schedule a day early or staying a day late to take in the sights of the town or go to a health spa.

Sometimes I visit my cousin's home, which is about a 40-mile drive from me, for over-night pajama parties where the two of us stay up late reminiscing, get up early, have a fourth or fifth cup of tea, shop, have a long lunch, and return home to our lives refreshed. This mini-vacation lasts a day and a half and is of low expense. Other ways I maintain my mental health are by taking a half day for a matinee and eating an early leisurely dinner with a colleague or a friend.

One of my male coaching clients spends one week each year with four college buddies who now live in different states. All are MBAs who use the time not only to refresh their friendship but also to develop collaborations and referrals and provide updates on net-working benefits, many of which have become extremely lucrative. Another client and her friend host a weekend spa event where they chip in and hire a masseuse and someone to do facials and pedicures at one of their homes. These are low-cost getaways that may offer you many opportunities to build boards and network while you are relaxing.

A great way to connect with younger professionals is by inviting them to happy-hour networking events. A friend of mine hosts a "chat and chew" during happy hour, asking friends to attend and bring their younger colleagues. This is a great way to pay it forward and create opportunities for the next generation. It provides a means for you to catch up with your peers and have fun. These kinds of networking events produce a variety of col-laborations and potential board members for your VPBOD.

Developing your career with a Personal Board is not a continuous, linear process; there will be stages where you have more or less time to yourself. During growth phases, when you are incredibly busy and under a lot of pressure, use your Personal Wellness Plan (PWP) to remind yourself to take time out to go to the gym, attend a yoga class, or listen to a meditation recording. When you are in a more established, less stressful phase of your career development, your PWP will focus more on connecting to your inner self and maintaining a mental sense of peace and well-being.

In order to be your best self, you have to take care of yourself on every level. Your Health & Wellness Experts are your go-to people for questions regarding not only your physical well-being, but also your mental and spiritual health. A PWP will be your guide in every aspect of your well-being. The following checklists give ideas for how to be your healthiest:

MAINTAIN TIP-TOP HEALTH

✓ Physically
✓ Mentally
✓ Spiritually

AVOID COMMON PITFALLS

- ✓ Compassion fatigue
- ✓ Burnout
- ✓ Lack of enjoyment of your work
- ✓ Low energy
- ✓ Poor health

WELLNESS MAINTENANCE CHECKLISTS

To maintain physical health:

- ✓ Schedule yearly general physical examinations.
- ✓ Follow up on any health issues.
- ✓ Have regular dental checkups.
- ✓ Follow a nutritional diet.
- ✓ Set aside time for enjoyable physical activity three to five times per week.

To maintain mental health:

- ✓ Do not work to avoid your personal life.
- ✓ Think about what brings you joy in life.
- ✓ Think about people who matter, family and friends.
- ✓ Make time to nourish a love life.
- ✓ Improve the quality of relationships at work.
- ✓ Set boundaries at the workplace.
- ✓ Arrange your office or workspace the best way for your mental health.
- ✓ Have an hour during the day when you are not taking calls.

To maintain spiritual health:

- ✓ Meditate.
- ✓ Pray.
- ✓ Practice yoga.
- ✓ Enjoy solitude.
- ✓ Think and reflect.
- ✓ Enjoy intimacy with loved ones.

FAMOUS MENTORING PAIRS: INTELLECTUALS, SCIENTISTS, ACADEMICS, AND TEACHERS

Mentor	Mentee
Josef Breuer, Austrian physician, developed the "talking cure"	Sigmund Freud, father of psychoanalysis
Jean-Martin Charcot, founder of clinical neurology	Sigmund Freud, father of psychoanalysis
John Dewey, US philosopher	George R. Geiger, Antioch psychology professor
Havelock Ellis, physician, psychologist, author	Margaret Sanger, pioneer activist for birth control
Sigmund Freud, father of psychoanalysis	Carl Gustav Jung, founder of analytical psychology
G. I. Gurdjieff, Russian philosopher	William Charles Segal, painter
Zellig Harris, US linguist	Noam Chomsky, US political activist
Frederich von Hayek, Austrian economist	Jimmy Lai, Hong Kong e-business billionaire
George Stigler, Nobel Prize winner in economics	Gary Becker, Nobel Prize winner in economics
Anne Sullivan, US teacher	Helen Keller, US author, political activist, and lecturer

PROFILES IN MENTORSHIP: SIGMUND FREUD AND CARL GUSTAV JUNG

When Protégés Do Not Follow the Mentor's Path

Sigmund Freud is well known as the mentor to fellow psychoanalyst Carl Gustav Jung. Although there was a mutual respect and a long-standing relationship, Jung eventually completely diverged from his mentor's theories and practice and set forth on his own professional path, based on his individual philosophies and unique concepts. In fact, Freudian psychology is often considered the direct opposite of Jungian psychology, a fact that may be considered ironic when one considers the mentoring relationship between the two pioneers in the field of psychology.

In fact, at the point at which the protégé set forth by pursuing his own ideas that radically differed from those of his mentor, there occurred a dramatic break in the relationship of the two men. When a mentee decides to forge his or her own path, a mentor may become insulted by the former student's rejection of his or her theories and ideas. It is not always the case that when a protégé pioneers his or her own distinct professional path, a mentor becomes embittered and aggressive. However, the well-documented and public break between Freud and Jung imparts important lessons about the potential pitfalls of a dyadic, monogamous mentor-protégé relationship.

KNOWLEDGE NUGGETS

- Building a Virtual Person Board of Directors is like cultivating a garden: you must first prepare and till the soil, which corresponds to the initial self-reflection and goal-setting process.
- Achieving expertise in building and leveraging the resources of a VPBOD takes patience, persistence, and dedication.
- Maintaining multiple relationships with a large number of professional colleagues is fundamental to cultivating a smoothly and effectively functioning Personal Board.
- For every move you make in your career, you need to reassess your relationships with board members, because every new move requires that you shift those relationships.
- Maintaining your Personal Board becomes just another aspect of maintaining yourself—and your health—once you have fully and seamlessly integrated your VPBOD into the functioning of your life.

> Patience, persistence and perspiration make an unbeatable combination for success.
>
> Napoleon Hill

CHAPTER 9

BUILDING A *NET* THAT *WORKS*

You don't need just a network. You need a NET that WORKS.

Ron Chisom

Networking is the most significant and pervasive conceptual framework on which the Virtual Personal Board of Directors methodology is based. Throughout all stages of the board-building process and the journey toward your professional best self, networking is *the* primary means of achieving professional success. In fact, a VPBOD, in its most basic form, *is* a personal network. But it is not just any network: a VPBOD is a developmental network, a network constructed for the express purpose of developing and cultivating professional success. A developmental network is defined as "a set of relationships an individual has with people who take an active interest in and action to advance the individual's career by assisting with his or her personal and professional development" (Higgins & Thomas, 2001, p. 223).

Networking is the driving engine that powers your Virtual Personal Board, that gets your wagon wheel in motion—and keeps it moving. You network to identify potential board members; you network to establish mentoring relationships; and then, once your Personal Board is built, you network with your board members and with *their* professional contacts. In order to build, leverage, and maintain a Virtual Personal Board, you must be an effective networker.

Merriam-Webster's defines networking as "the exchange of information or services among individuals, groups, or institutions; *specifically* the cultivation of productive relationships for employment or business" (www.merriam-webster.com). The two most important phrases in this definition are "exchange of information" and "cultivation of productive relationships." These two elements of networking are also at the core of the VPBOD methodology and are inextricably linked: you network in order to build your Personal Board, and you build your Personal Board in order to network.

NETWORKING TO CULTIVATE PRODUCTIVE RELATIONSHIPS

You can't be your best self by yourself. Everyone needs the support of family, friends, colleagues, and others to become his or her best self. The goal is to have everything you need in your network, and it is possible to do that by growing the *net* to ensure that it *works*. If you maintain your network properly, you will know where the gaps are and work on filling in those specific areas.

> Networking with integrity creates a greater willingness of all parties to be part of a human conduit to serve as energy and resource to one another. Sometimes you will give more than you receive and sometimes you will get back more than you give. It's not about keeping score.
>
> Chris London

You have to constantly work on your relationships with your board members. You also need to feel that people are interested in you and have a genuine affinity with the people in your network. Any relationship, whether personal or professional, is a constant give and take. Your relationships with your mentors should not be tit-for-tat, where you do something for them in exchange for what they do for you, or vice versa. When you give a certain person a lot of help, you should not feel as if that person "owes" you. You will be "repaid" for the help you have given others, but to whom you give is not necessarily from whom you shall receive. You work with individual mentors in order to build equity with your network as a whole. You are investing in your entire network with each and every action you take for any individual in that network. And your network *will* yield profits in the long term if you stick with it and continue to invest in it with your time and effort. As you build equity with individuals in your network, you will have more assets to leverage and thus more resources at your disposal with which you can advance your career.

> Your power is almost directly proportional to the thickness of your Rolodex, and the time you spend maintaining it. Put bluntly, the most potent people I've known have been the best networkers—they "know everybody from everywhere" and have just been out to lunch with most of them.
>
> Tom Peters

NETWORKING TO EXCHANGE OR ACQUIRE INFORMATION

There is another special advantage to having a developmental network like a VPBOD at your disposal: the ability to quickly acquire vital information with the minimum of effort.

There are times when you encounter a situation in which you require the advice or guidance of an experienced professional in order to make a decision. You can acquire information from individual mentors on a one-on-one basis; for example, you might need an ISP for your website, so you can call on one of your CTOs for a recommendation. But you can also mine your network as a whole to find information for which you don't already have a resource on your board.

NETWORKING MODALITIES

There are many different ways to network: in person, via social media, via e-mail, with your own website, and via phone and mail. Each networking modality has its advantages and disadvantages It is important to know which method to use in various situations in order to maximize the effectiveness of your networking efforts.

Networking has never been easier than since the advent of the World Wide Web. Today you can make new connections you never could have made 20 years ago, because the person you want to meet has a presence online and is therefore accessible to you. It hasn't always been this easy to get in touch with just about anyone. Ambitious professionals can use this to their advantage in reaching out to potential clients, customers, employers, and contacts as never before.

By the same token, the Internet has led to information overload in many ways. It is important to learn how to manage the Internet in an efficient manner in order to control it and not become controlled by it. Of the five networking modalities listed below, three are Internet-related. This is indicative of just how influential and important the Internet has become in our business communications. However, it is important to remember that networking in person, such as at industry events and conferences, and keeping in touch with phone calls and letters are also very important ways to network. The key is to know which method to choose in order to maximize the likelihood of achieving the desired outcome. It takes time, practice, and experience to become an effective networker, so don't become discouraged if you aren't able to achieve your most ambitious connections on your first try.

NETWORKING WITH SOCIAL MEDIA

One of the primary ways to network online is to follow blogs and websites featuring individuals in whom you are interested. Gather information and ideas from these websites and blogs. Focus on identifying new trends in your field, because your options may have expanded; there may be new things happening that interest you of which you are not yet aware. Comment on colleagues' blogs and articles as a means of forging and deepening these relationships. Consider the possibility of guest blogging, starting your own blog, or contributing articles to leading industry websites or publications. This is a proactive way to contribute to the industry conversation, get noticed by colleagues, and make new connections.

And last, but definitely not least, no online networking strategy would be complete without representation on social networking sites such as Twitter, Facebook, and LinkedIn. Subscribe to the blogs of colleagues you admire, follow them on Twitter and LinkedIn, and attend online events, such as Livestream lectures they are appearing in, to demonstrate your interest in their work. The goal is to expand your network.

NETWORKING BY E-MAIL

E-mail is a networker's best friend. It is an easy, unobtrusive, accessible, and effective means of communicating with almost anyone. E-mail is an appropriate way to contact your best friend, your doctor, your boss, your babysitter, your friend from college—in short, it is acceptable and appropriate to e-mail just about anyone with whom you want to communicate. This makes it the most versatile and useful tool in your networking toolbox. E-mail should be considered the default communication modality for keeping in touch with board members.

One of the most important aspects of an e-mail is the subject line. Think of it as the headline for your e-mail; when you are reading a newspaper, you read the stories whose headlines grab your attention, and your subject lines should do the same. Your e-mail should be short, direct, and to the point. If it is an invitation to an industry event, you should say so in the subject line and include all necessary information in as few words as possible. Choose when you send e-mails strategically. On Monday morning, everyone's inbox is often full of actionable work-related e-mails. The best time to send a "Hello, let's become friends" e-mail is on a Wednesday or Thursday afternoon, as the week is winding down, and the recipient is likely to have fewer unopened work-related e-mails in his or her inbox. Furthermore, never send a group e-mail that shows the recipients' addresses; always blind-copy the group.

NETWORKING WITH A PERSONAL WEBSITE

You do not always have to be in pursuit of other people when networking. One way you can get contacts to come to you is to maintain a web presence not only with social media but also with a personal website or web blog. Although doing so takes some effort, it is an extremely important tool in your networking toolbox. You may have to turn to your Chief Technical Officers for advice if you are not an Internet maven, but it is well worth the time.

Your personal website is the place where you will establish who you are and what you do with a bio, résumé, press clippings, and, of course, contact information. Try to use the domain name of your full name, such as www.marypendergreene.com, or some variation thereof, so that when someone Googles you, your site is the top match and the first place people will go to find out about you. This way, *you* get the first word in the conversation about who you are with any potential board member, client, or colleague. Another important online networking strategy is to manage your search-engine presence by increasing the Google hits on your name and managing their rankings.

Your personal website may be static, that is, unchanging, or it may be dynamic, that is, constantly updated. There are ways to automate new content to appear on your website on a regular basis to give people a reason to come back again and again; for example, you can syndicate content from a colleague or organization you admire and respect and in which visitors to your site are likely to be interested.

NETWORKING OLD-SCHOOL
BY MAIL AND TELEPHONE

Sometimes sending a physical piece of mail rather than an ephemeral e-mail is the best way to get someone's attention. Letters stand out, because more people use e-mail to communicate today. For example, if a board member gifts you an eIntroduction to a much-sought-after Professional Guru in your field, instead of just expressing your gratitude via e-mail, take the time to handwrite a personal thank-you note and mail it to his or her place of business. In fact, investing in a box of quality thank-you notes is a good idea; this way, you always have one on hand. Sending a thank-you card or a letter takes effort and also adds a personal touch that will leave a lasting impression on your mentor.

Telephone calls are another old-school way of networking that should be reserved for special circumstances. You should only call board members when it is absolutely imperative that you speak to them. In addition, you should only call mentors with whom you have already established a rapport and a real relationship. It is not recommended to call potential board members, Members-at-Large, or someone brand-new to your Personal Board out of the blue. Wait until you have established tangible ties with board members, and let *them* call *you* before you start initiating phone communication.

NETWORKING IN PERSON

When you are networking in person, at conferences, workshops, or other events, your aim is to meet new people and make connections. Find out where colleagues with common objectives to your own get together, either for business or pleasure. If you go to an event, you should dress professionally in order to make a good first impression. Avoid situations where you might be uncomfortable in a social situation; for example, don't bring a heavy bag to a formal event. No matter what your financial situation, make sure your wardrobe contains at least one appropriate outfit that enhances your physical appearance and boosts your confidence. Your first interaction with others goes a long way to determining their ultimate opinion of you.

When engaging with new acquaintances at an event, have meaningful conversations about relevant topics. Don't interrupt a discussion in progress or be too aggressive when speaking; you learn more by simply listening. Try not to gravitate toward the people you already know at any given event; doing so will preclude you from mingling and meeting new people.

Before you go to an event, draw up a list of people you want to meet. Whether it is a networking reception or a professional conference, upon entering, you should scan the room for people you want to meet. If you get caught up in any negative situations or cornered by negative individuals, politely excuse yourself and move on. Ask people questions rather than talking about yourself. You should try to meet at least five new people at each industry or work event. Become familiar with the hosts, and be sure to thank them for their hospitality. Ask any new acquaintances who spark your interest for their business cards, and make notes so you can remember them.

When you get a business card, follow up within 24 hours to ensure that your new contact remembers you and keeps you on his or her radar. If you give out cards, you need to reach out to your contacts. Make them interested in you; one way to do that is simply to keep the lines of communication open by staying in contact. Note on the back of the card (or on the VPBOD system app online at www.VirtualPersonalBoard.com) where, when, and how you met this individual and the key points about him or her that caught your attention.

If you feel anxious about interacting with other people, Toastmasters International will help you feel more comfortable and is an excellent venue for networking and locating board members. Toastmasters International is an extremely low-cost nonprofit educational organization that operates clubs worldwide for the purpose of helping members improve their communication, public-speaking, and leadership skills. Through its thousands of member clubs, Toastmasters International offers a program of communication and leadership projects designed to help people learn the arts of speaking, listening, and thinking.

PLACES TO NETWORK: NATIONAL CONFERENCES, WORKSHOPS, OR LECTURES

Attending the national conferences of your profession is one way to find new potential board members and network with professional colleagues. When you attend a national conference, you should scan the brochure and find workshops that interest you; you may become acquainted with potential board members in these workshops—perhaps the keynote speaker, perhaps a fellow attendee; you never know where you will encounter someone with whom you click immediately. Not every workshop attendee or speaker will be appointed to your board, but they could be prospects.

You should also join the national professional association for your industry so that you receive the newsletters and have access to the specialized information they provide for members only. "Joining networks of various kinds can expand one's options. . . . Networks allow individuals to meet others who have similar professional concerns. Relationships in these contexts often provide several career or psychosocial functions; they can offer, for example, information sharing, career strategizing, emotional support, and friendship" (Kram, 1985, pp. 156–157).

Celebratory events for colleagues and coworkers are perfect places to expand your Personal Board by networking with interesting people. The mood is usually light and merry, making for easy conversation. Events such as book publication parties, openings, promotions, and seminars give you great opportunities to network in a fun environment.

PROSPECTING FOR BOARD MEMBERS BY NETWORKING

> Networking is marketing. Marketing yourself, marketing your uniqueness, marketing what you stand for.
>
> Christine Comaford-Lynch

It is scary to meet with a variety of people you don't know. People fear rejection or worry that they will not be respected for who they are. You are trying to find an area of focus by looking at a wide array of things and then narrowing down what you are interested in. You should look at where you are already good at something. You should also look at internships, workshops, audio books, or anything that will expand your perspective and provide additional information. The more knowledge you have, the more options are available to you. Ask yourself: "What is it that is unique about me? What is it that really makes me feel good? What have people told me I am good at? What kind of people do I enjoy working with?" It is important not to keep your talents a secret, especially not from yourself. When you meet with board prospects, it is not a time to be modest. It is not about bragging, but you should highlight what your strengths are. You want to be able to articulate what you have passion for and what you are able to do. The more people you meet with, the stronger your vision will become. Develop an elevator speech.

As mentioned earlier, an elevator speech is a short summary used to quickly and simply define a person, profession, product, service, organization, or event and its value proposition. It reflects the idea that it should be possible to deliver the summary in the time span of an elevator ride, approximately 30 seconds to two minutes. It comes from a scenario of an accidental meeting with someone important in the elevator. If the conversation inside the elevator in those few seconds is interesting and value-adding, the conversation may continue after the elevator ride, ending in an exchange of business cards or a scheduled meeting.

USING YOUR VIRTUAL PERSONAL BOARD AS A NETWORK

> The currency of real networking is not greed but generosity.
>
> Keith Ferrazzi

A VPBOD is a powerful asset to have in your professional portfolio, which will enable you to advance your career and achieve your professional goals. In chapter 8, we discussed how to leverage your Personal Board in many different ways: to find a job, to learn new skills, to get a different perspective on a situation. The ways you can leverage your VPBOD are innumerable—it is up to you how far you choose to take it. However, the most important way you can leverage its resources is by using your Personal Board specifically as a developmental network, a pool of people you can turn to in order to accomplish any number of objectives. While the one-on-one mentoring aspects of your relationships with board members are very important, you should also visualize the board as an entity unto itself: your professional posse. This perspective will enable you to take how you use your board to the next level. Utilizing your Personal Board as a network yields a whole new set of applications and benefits.

Like a cooperative ("co-op"), a professional posse is an autonomous association of persons who voluntarily cooperate for their mutual, social, economic, and cultural benefit (as defined on Wikipedia). The major issue with the cooperative or the professional posse is that you cannot participate in it and receive its benefits without making your own contributions of time and energy.

You pay for entry with your time, advice, attention, and influence, and you are making this all available to your specific professional posse, which therefore gives you access to the time, advice, attention, and influence of everyone not only in your network but in *their* networks. The influence of your network increases by orders of magnitude exponentially with effort and over time.

TO SOLVE PROBLEMS

Now that you have a professional posse at your disposal, solving problems becomes much easier, not only from a practical standpoint but also from a psychological one. You know that you are not facing this problem alone—you have a group of people whom you can depend on for not only guidance and advice but also emotional support. You exponentially increase your problem-solving ability by pooling the resources of your board members into a cohesive developmental network, thereby giving yourself access to all of their combined experience, expertise, and effort. There are many issues we are forced to face and address on our own, but there are also problems that lend themselves to a network-oriented solution.

For example, an entrepreneur, Soledad, is running a small catering business. She finds herself in a situation where she suddenly needs to fill an order that requires five extra employees—but only for one day. Because she is just starting out, her operating budget is stretched to the limit, and she does not have the overhead to cover hiring five extra people even for one hour, much less an entire day. Filling this order is crucial: not only would the profit cover her expenses for the entire month, but this client regularly places orders of this size, so acing this one order could potentially mean a permanent expansion of Soledad's business. What does she do?

Well, if she has a professional posse, she mines her network for five people who are willing to work for one day for deferred payment. It most likely won't be board members who end up doing the job, but when Soledad puts the word out to her posse, they will mine their own networks for appropriate individuals to fill the need. A peer mentor who is considering becoming a caterer may volunteer so she can learn by doing. Soledad's sponsor may send her teenage son, who is home from college for the summer, to work for the day because she is invested in seeing her sponsee succeed. Another board member may have a mentee who is looking for an internship in the food service industry and recommend that she help Soledad. Without a professional posse to depend on, Soledad would have either had to go into debt to pay high hourly wages to last-minute temps or chance going it alone, delivering a mediocre service, and missing out on a career-changing opportunity.

TO ACCOMPLISH A FEAT

Having a professional posse at your disposal makes purpose-oriented networking, that is, consulting large numbers of people in order to accomplish a specific task, easier to do and also increases the likelihood that you will achieve more daunting tasks with less effort. For example, say you want to get on the board of directors for the Ford Foundation. If you have no connections, this is a goal that will be a challenge to achieve. By cultivating your professional posse with extensive connections, you increase your chances of having someone in your network who will know someone who knows someone who can provide you with the needed connection.

TO INCREASE YOUR VISIBILITY

Every professional—not only entrepreneurs—has to constantly market himself or herself in the current employment environment. Even if you are comfortable in your current career, consider ways to increase your visibility. And if you are running your own business, self-promotion is absolutely essential to guaranteeing a steady stream of business. Your professional posse is an extensive network of contacts who are constantly on the lookout for jobs for you. Not only will they help you professionally by recommending potential clients and jobs to you, but they will also think of you when they see a job come up in which you might be interested. There is no type of marketing as cost-effective and successful as word-of-mouth recommendation, and with a professional posse, you will be able to increase your visibility and maintain a presence among your professional circle.

TO FIND AN EMPLOYEE

Having a Personal Board is an enormous asset when looking to fill an open position. Being able to put the word out to your developmental network is likely to yield more than a few qualified candidates. Your VPBOD members will mine their networks for individuals they know are looking for a position such as the one for which you are hiring and recommend that they send you their résumés. The more contacts you have on your Personal

Board, the more likely one of your board members or someone in his or her network will know someone who is qualified for that position.

TO FIND A NEW JOB

Your Personal Board will prove to be crucial when it comes to finding a job. Whether you are rewiring after being laid off, you've been downsized in mid-career, or you are a recent college graduate looking for your first entry-level position, your Personal Board can help you.

CONNECTORS

According to Malcolm Gladwell, author of *The Tipping Point* (Gladwell, 2002), connectors are individuals who have ties in many different realms and act as conduits between them, helping to engender connections, relationships, and "cross-fertilization" that otherwise might not have ever occurred. "What makes someone a connector? The first—and most obvious—criterion is that connectors know a lot of people. They are the kinds of people that know everyone" (Gladwell, 2002, p. 38). Your goal in your networking is to cultivate relationships with as many connectors as possible. By stacking your Personal Board with connectors, you will ensure that no matter whom you meet—whether from a different industry, a different profession, or a different country—you will be able to track someone down through your network. "Sprinkled among every walk of life, in other words, are a handful of people with a truly extraordinary knack of making friends and acquaintances. They are connectors" (Gladwell, 2002, p. 42).

Connectors make your network more versatile, because they know lots of people from all walks of life, and they enjoy bringing people together. "The point about a Connector is that by having a foot in so many different worlds they have the effect of bringing them all together" (Gladwell, 2002, p. 51). How can you identify a connector? Most likely, he or she will display a very outgoing personality and be extremely well-liked and popular and have a lot of friends, contacts, and acquaintances. In addition, "in case of Connectors, their ability to span many different worlds is a function of something intrinsic to their personality, some combination of curiosity, self-confidence, sociability, and energy" (Gladwell, 2002, p. 46). Having connectors in your network will enable you to reach out and connect with people in completely different fields and professions and from totally different circles from those you frequent, putting more diverse resources at your disposal.

CULTIVATING CAREER CAPITAL
WITH YOUR PERSONAL BOARD

One way a Personal Board is maintained is by building capital with your board members in terms of investing in the relationship. By doing things for your mentor or someone in his or her network, however small, over time, you will find that you build capital with the mentor that you can leverage at a later date and that sets you apart from other mentees or protégés with whom he or she may be working.

> First, our study found that mentoring added value, above and beyond the other forms of career capital, in predicting promotion, advancement expectations and turnover intentions and that mentoring mattered more than human, agentic, or developmental network capital in predicting promotion and advancement expectations. A key principle of mentoring theory is that mentors help their protégés advance (Kram, 1985), and the present study confirmed this important function.

However, emerging perspectives hold that individuals can acquire other developmental relationships and "career communities" that may influence career success (Higgins & Kram, 2001; Parker, Arthur & Inkson, 2004). These relationships involve peers and senior colleagues who do not serve as mentors but rather offer career encouragement and support that may be periodic and focused on a particular job function. Although these individuals would not view their relationship as a mentoring relationship, they would nevertheless acknowledge its value in offering periodic episodes of career support and encouragement (see Fletcher & Ragins, 2007). We call this type of career capital "developmental network capital," and we define it as relational career resources embedded within communities of work relationships that provide encouragement and career support.

FAMOUS MENTORING PAIRS: ENTERTAINMENT II—
MUSICIANS, WRITERS, AND ARTISTS

Mentor	Mentee
Johann Sebastian Bach, German composer	Wolfgang Amadeus Mozart, German composer
Mariah Carey, US singer-songwriter	Christina Aguilera, US recording artist
Ray Charles, US singer-songwriter	Quincy Jones, US record producer
Jimmy Cliff, Jamaican musician	Bob Marley, Jamaican musician
Patsy Cline, US country music singer	Loretta Lynn, US country music singer-songwriter
Bing Crosby, US singer and actor	Frank Sinatra, US singer and actor
Clive Davis, US record producer	Whitney Houston, US singer
Miles Davis, US jazz musician	John Coltrane, US jazz musician
Duke Ellington, US jazz composer	Tony Bennett, US jazz singer
Dizzy Gillespie, US jazz musician	Hugh Masekela, South African trumpeter
Whitney Houston, US recording artist	Brandy, US recording artist
Fat Joe, US rapper	Big Pun, US rapper
Madonna, US singer-songwriter	Gwyneth Paltrow, US actress
Wynton Marsalis, US jazz musician	Harry Connick Jr., US actor and musician
Max Martin, —Swedish music producer	Britney Spears, —US recording artist
Reba McEntire, US country music singer-songwriter	Martina McBride, US country music singer-songwriter
Charlie Parker, US jazz musician	Max Roach, US jazz musician
Carl Perkins, US rockabilly musician	George Harrison, UK musician
Ma Rainey, US blues singer	Bessie Smith, US blues singer
Ravi Shankar, Indian musician and composer	George Harrison, UK musician
Tina Turner, US singer	Mick Jagger, UK singer-songwriter

PROFILES IN MENTORSHIP: ART BLAKEY—JAZZ MESSENGER, JAZZ MENTOR

The great drummer and bandleader Art Blakey was one of the most important mentors in jazz history. For more than 30 years from the mid-1950s until his death in 1990, his group the Jazz Messengers served as a graduate school and a springboard for some of the most influential jazz musicians. Most of the individuals whom he mentored through the the Jazz Messengers became some of the greatest jazz players of all time. The list of those who played in his group either as guests or as permanent members reads like a Who's Who of great jazz musicians: Miles Davis, Charlie Parker, Lee Morgan, Hank Mobley, Wayne Shorter, Bobby Watson, Donald Byrd, Curtis Fuller, Johnny Griffin, Benny Golson, Freddie Hubbard, Keith Jarrett, Woody Shaw, Joanne Brackeen, James Williams, and three of the Marsalis brothers (Wynton, Branford, and Delfeayo).

KNOWLEDGE NUGGETS

- Throughout all stages of the board-building process and the journey toward your professional best self, networking is *the* primary means of achieving professional success.
- It is important to know which networking modality to use in various situations in order to maximize the effectiveness of your networking efforts.
- When you meet with board prospects, it is not a time to be modest. Highlight what your strengths and passions are.
- The most important way you can leverage your Personal Board's resources is by using it specifically as a developmental network, a pool of people you can turn to in order to accomplish any number of objectives.
- Your professional posse, which gives you access to the time, advice, attention, and influence of everyone in your network and in your mentors' networks. The influence of your network increases by orders of magnitude exponentially with effort and over time.
- Having connectors in your network will enable you to reach out and connect with people in completely different fields and professions and from totally different circles from those you frequent, putting more diverse resources at your disposal.
- By doing things for your mentor or someone in his or her network, however small, over time, you will find that you build capital with the mentor that you can leverage at a later date.

CHAPTER 10

SERVING ON A PERSONAL BOARD

I've learned that people will forget what you said, people will forget what you did, but people will never forget how you made them feel.

Maya Angelou

Do not make the mistake of thinking that once you have achieved your vision of your best self with the help of your Virtual Personal Board of Directors, your job is over or that you will no longer need to rely on it for professional guidance and support. As we have stated, the board-building process is *never* complete; you will have to maintain your VPBOD garden constantly throughout your career. In addition, your participation with, use of, and responsibility for your Personal Board does not end with the accomplishment of your ultimate goal, nor does it end with retirement. In fact, in the late career phase, once you have achieved your highest professional aspirations, or in the post-career, when you retire, you should engage with your Personal Board as much as possible. However, your focus will be not on seeking advice and guidance from your own mentors but, rather, paying it forward by serving on colleagues' Personal Boards and embracing the role of mentor and board member for others.

In the late career phase and beyond, you have more time to guide and advise mentees. In addition, as a seasoned, accomplished professional in your field, you are in an ideal position to mentor others; you possess more influence to wield on their behalf and have access to potentially helpful colleagues in the profession and a comprehensive contact database. The combination of these two assets—extra time and increased resources—makes your service on Personal Boards easier than ever before. You are also most effective in this phase of your career because of all your resources. Therefore, you are able most effectively to assist your mentees and guide them on the path to success.

WHY SHOULD YOU BECOME A MENTOR?

The true meaning of life is to plant trees, under whose shade you do not expect to sit.

Nelson Henderson

One reason you may want to be on a protégé's board is that you want to preserve or carry on your legacy. If you know someone you think will be able to carry on your legacy, you want to be on their board to influence that person. If you are rewiring/retiring, you want someone you know who is qualified to replace your position on the board. Before leaving a board in which you have been a member for 20 years, you will be able to suggest a replacement with your mentee. By serving on people's boards, you will preserve the work you have done over time, ensuring that you have successors with the knowledge and perspective that you strived for throughout your career. You will be able to step away with confidence from projects you started, because your mentees will be able to move them to new heights.

HOW TO CHOOSE WHOSE BOARDS TO SERVE ON

The choice of a board to serve on depends on the following factors:

- Your career phase and stage.
- Your industry.
- What you need from mentees. (Do you need fresh young thinkers to assist you with new ideas? Do you need to be more connected to your industry?)

WORKSHEET: AM I READY TO MENTOR?

Respond yes or no to the following. Give yourself a score of 1 for yes and 0 for no.

- I am in a middle-management, directorial, or executive role at my organization.
- I am well known among my colleagues and have a wide array of professional contacts.
- Both subordinates and peers seek me out for guidance and advice about our field.
- I enjoy giving advice to subordinates, peers, and new entrants to my field.
- I speak at industry events, professional conferences, and board meetings or other professional gatherings.
- I take pleasure in helping others succeed in their goals.
- I have groomed a protégé and mentored subordinates before.
- I have always wanted to be a mentor to someone.
- I am very grateful to the mentors in my life who helped me achieve my professional goals.

If you received a score of 5 or higher, you are ready to become a mentor.

CHARACTERISTICS OF A POSITIVE MENTEE RELATIONSHIP

You both feel as though you are getting satisfaction and enjoyment from the relationship.

- The mentee is very respectful of your privacy and does not make excessive demands on your time.
- The mentee is respectful, has decorum, and is trustworthy.
- The mentee is motivated and dedicated to professional advancement through a Personal Board.
- The mentee is prepared for meetings, asks questions, takes notes, and follows through on your advice and guidance.
- The mentee voices disagreement with your opinions or advice and is honest, straightforward, truthful, up-front.

CHARACTERISTICS OF A NEGATIVE MENTEE RELATIONSHIP

- The mentee is co-dependent or too dependent on you.
- The mentee demands too much time from you.
- The mentee is uncommitted and unmotivated to do the work.
- The mentee does not follow instructions and guidance.
- The mentee comes to you for advice but rarely takes it or follows through on it.
- The mentee may be insincere.
- The mentee expects too much too soon.
- The mentee is untrustworthy and lacks discretion.
- You are too emotionally attached to the mentee, and you lack an unbiased perspective.
- You feel unfairly obligated to perform mentoring role and feel resentful.
- The mentee does not respect your boundaries—physical, professional, or emotional.

THE BENEFITS OF MENTORING

1. Preserving your professional legacy into the future by instilling your values into future generations.
2. Maintaining your political influence on the future development of your profession and your field.
3. Maintaining visibility in your field.
4. Influencing the future of your profession.
5. Staying connected with younger generations, the future of your profession.
6. Learning new things about your profession. Younger mentees will be able to keep you apprised of new developments.
7. Learning new things about your field. You will keep up to date on cutting-edge developments.
8. Encouraging and cultivating continuity of knowledge and best practices in your profession.
9. Fostering a culture of generosity and sharing. By giving your time to subordinates and colleagues, by serving on their Personal Boards or simply as their mentor, you are encouraging them.
10. Setting an example for peers, subordinates, and higher-ups. Mentoring and serving on Personal Boards are responsibilities that are not required of you. Therefore, by giving your time and effort selflessly to assist colleagues and subordinates, by sharing knowledge, experience, and information, you provide an example for your coworkers, higher-ups, and subordinates. You may inspire peers and higher-ups to follow suit and also be mentors, a you may provide a positive role model for subordinates.

RULES OF ENGAGEMENT: SERVING ON A VIRTUAL PERSONAL BOARD

Rule 1. Never ask people if they would like you to be their mentor. Encourage mentees to seek you out by being open, interested, and responsive to subordinates and younger colleagues. Expressing curiosity is key to attracting potential mentees.

Rule 2. Serving on the boards of coworkers and colleagues as a peer mentor is just as important as cultivating younger subordinates.

Rule 3. Do not focus all your mentoring energy on a single protégé; spread your time among many mentees so that you can help as many people as possible.

Rule 4. Don't foster dependency on one person.

Rule 5. Do not expect your mentees to do busy work or otherwise serve you in exchange for your time.

Rule 6. Teach the VPBOD system to all of your mentees, and encourage them to create their own boards.

SERVING ON A VPBOD THROUGHOUT YOUR CAREER

At each successive phase of your career—even the initial establishment phase—you are fully capable of serving on others' Virtual Personal Boards, and you should make an effort to do so as soon as you feel comfortable. Despite the fact that the VPBOD arrangement is informal, it is easy to tell when a colleague appoints you to his or her board. Below is a summary of how you can serve on Personal Board at each stage of your career:

ESTABLISHMENT CAREER PHASE

- As a peer mentor.
- As a Big Brother/Big Sister volunteer in the local community.
- As a mentor to younger family members.
- As a mentor to college and high school students.

ADVANCEMENT CAREER PHASE

- As a peer mentor.

MIDDLE CAREER PHASE

- As a boss-mentor.
- As a peer mentor.

LATE CAREER PHASE

- As a Professional Guru.
- As a boss-mentor.

FAMOUS MENTORING PAIRS: PHILANTHROPISTS, SOCIAL WORKERS, AND ACTIVISTS

Mentor	Mentee
Samuel C. Armstrong, founder of Hampton University	Booker T. Washington, African-American educator and civil rights leader
John P. Altgeld, Illinois governor	Clarence Darrow, leading member of the American Civil Liberties Union
Eugene V. Debs, union leader and labor activist	John Gardner, US novelist and professor
Raymond B. Fosdick, president of the Rockefeller Foundation	John D. Rockefeller, business mogul and philanthropist
Mahatma Gandhi, Indian leader	Martin Luther King, Jr., African-American civil rights leader
William Lloyd Garrison, abolitionist	Frederick Douglass, African-American leader
Lillie Carroll Jackson, US women's rights and civil rights activist	Thurgood Marshall, US Supreme Court justice
Jim Hayes, community activist	Ron Chisom, antiracism activist
Martin Luther King, Jr., African-American civil rights leader	Jesse Jackson, African-American civil rights leader
Martin Luther King, Jr., African-American civil rights leader	John Lewis, African-American civil rights leader
Jean Marchand, Quebec labor leader	Pierre Elliott Trudeau, Canadian prime minister
Benjamin Mays, president of Morehouse College	Martin Luther King, Jr., African-American civil rights leader
Elizabeth Cady Stanton, US social activist and abolitionist	Susan B. Anthony, US civil rights leader and feminist
Victor Raúl Haya de la Torre, Peruvian political activist	Alan García Pérez, president of Peru
Mercy Otis Warren, US propagandist of the American Revolution	Abigail Adams, US first lady
Booker T. Washington, African-American educator and civil rights leader	William Henry Holtzclaw, founder of the Utica Institute
Alice L. White, Rosa Parks's school principal	Rosa Parks, African-American civil rights activist
Malcolm X, African-American civil rights leader	Louis Farrakhan, African-American civil rights leader

PROFILES IN MENTORSHIP: ANDREW CARNEGIE AND NAPOLEON HILL

> No man is so foolish but he may sometimes give another good counsel, and no man so wise that he may not easily err if he takes no other counsel than his own—He that is taught only by himself has a fool as a master.
>
> Ben Johnson

Napoleon Hill is called the "mentor to the mentors of the world" because he was able, through the mentorship of Andrew Carnegie, to learn about certain principles that the steel magnate had used in order to build his empire, and he wrote about them in his seminal self-help books *Think and Grow Rich* (1937) and *Napoleon Hill's Keys to Success: The 17 Principles of Personal Achievement* (Hill, 1997). Principles such as "the mastermind alliance," "the organization of the science of success philosophy," and "definiteness of purpose" were only a few that Hill passed on to the world through his bestselling books.

Quotes from Napoleon Hill about Andrew Carnegie
Profile of Andrew Carnegie
Carnegie was born in very humble circumstances, so he knew firsthand what it was like to want for even the basic necessities of life. However, he did not allow circumstances to dictate the course of his life. He had little formal education. He was self-educated and was a strong proponent of education and reading. Carnegie knew from his own experience the price one must pay for personal achievement.

He worked as a laborer, so he knew what it was like to start at the bottom rung of the success ladder and work his way up. Carnegie certainly walked the talk.

He became the principle owner of U.S. Steel, and through his ability to gather key people with the skills and expertise he lacked, he built a very successful company. He was a successful leader of people.

Because of his financial savvy, he became one of the richest men in the world, a reported billionaire. Carnegie was prudent about with whom he shared his knowledge. He witnessed how these associates also achieved outstanding success in business and life. Their success provided preliminary confirmation of the validity of his formula and success system.

Wanting to contribute to the betterment of society, Carnegie provided generous donations to various causes, which is why his name appears on countless libraries throughout the country. He truly was a noble philanthropist.

He wanted this formula and system that he had used to raise himself from laborer to billionaire steel company owner taught in schools and colleges so that everyone could benefit from this knowledge. He was a true seeker and revealer of truth.

He gave Hill the opportunity to validate the universal authenticity of his formula by introducing him to 3,000 of the most successful men and women in the world, who would become candidates for Hill's research. Carnegie received no financial reward for assisting Hill with his research, which helped validate the trust he had earned with his associates, friends and peers.

Carnegie's background as the explorer, developer, and tester of his formula and success system and as mentor to Hill provides us with clues to the attributes and key qualities of a true mentor.

KNOWLEDGE NUGGETS

- You will constantly have to maintain your Virtual Personal Board of Directors garden throughout your career.
- You need to serve on people's boards in order to preserve the work you have done over time by ensuring that you have successors with the knowledge and perspective that you have strived for throughout your career.
- Do not focus all your mentoring energy on a single protégé; spread your time among many mentees so that you can help as many people as possible. Don't foster dependency by one person.
- Having positive relationships with your mentees is key. Be wary of negative characteristics, such as a mentee who is insincere or one who does not respect boundaries.

CONCLUSION

The Future of the Virtual Personal Board

The best way to predict the future is to create it.

Abraham Lincoln

New mentoring models, such as developmental networks theorized by Kathy Kram and relationship constellations put forth by Monica Higgins, address today's urgent need for inventive approaches to career development as a result of the challenges of a constantly shifting and comparatively unstable professional environment. The Virtual Personal Board of Directors approach to mentoring in this changing professional milieu is an example of a progressive and innovative method of promoting the continued cultivation of the ages-old institution of mentorship in contemporary professional culture. But the question now becomes how we, as a society, can inspire and motivate current and subsequent generations to adopt and implement these new mentoring methods in order to advance their careers. There are three different approaches to encourage the adoption and propagation of developmental networks such as the VPBOD:

1. A one-on-one approach.
2. An educational approach.
3. An organizational approach.

There are pros and cons to each of these approaches. Following are summaries of these three strategies to encourage the growth and spread of the VPBOD mentoring model. It is imperative that the concept of cultivating developmental networks must specifically be communicated and imparted to these populations:

1. Novice professionals who are facing difficult employment prospects in an exceedingly competitive work environment.

2. Seasoned and mature professionals in the process of **rewiring** and facing challenging transitions into new organizations, fields, and professions.
3. Students about to enter a workforce that is arduous to navigate.

What follows is a brief overview of various methods and more in-depth scholarly research for those who want to pursue further analysis of potential ways to advance the mentoring methodologies.

A ONE-ON-ONE APPROACH TO SPREADING THE VPBOD SYSTEM

A primary means of encouraging new mentoring methods such as the VPBOD is a one-on-one approach in which a family-member mentor or another close individual teaches friends and family about the benefits of the benefits of the VPBOD methodology. One of the best ways to do this is teaching by example and exposing young people to witnessing Personal Boards in action. Exposing young people to developmental networks illustrates the principle and helps inculcate the methods of building and using a VPBOD not only in their educational life but also their professional life down the road.

Another way to encourage the development of these life skills is for professionals at various stages of their careers to take on the mentoring of younger individuals in college, those just entering the workforce, and entry-level beginners by proactively seeking the forging of such relationships. They can do so at their places of business, whether for an organization or for their own entrepreneurial pursuits. In addition, volunteer opportunities at programs such as the YWCA, Boys and Girls Clubs, or Big Brothers/Big Sisters are rewarding ways to forge mentoring relationships for professionals who may work from home or run their own businesses and have difficulty encountering individuals with whom to encourage the development of mentoring relationships.

TEACHING THE VPBOD METHODOLOGY: AN EDUCATIONAL APPROACH

Another means of spreading the VPBOD methodology is through an educational approach. Integrating the basics of developmental network methodology into the curricula of all levels of the educational system, from high schools to the university level, and encouraging students not only to learn the principles of Personal Boards but also to learn how to implement these strategies in appropriate ways depending on their grade level will help foster the development of these skills in young people. This will ensure the propagation of the new mentoring that has been designed to accommodate the changes in the professional landscape that new professionals will have to face in the workplace.

MENTORSHIP TRAINING:
AN ORGANIZATIONAL APPROACH

Organizations can also start mentoring programs that encourage their employees to take advantage of their access to seasoned and experienced professionals. Many large corporations and organizations have recently established mentoring programs. However, participation should be voluntary, and mentors and mentees should find one another organically, rather than being assigned to one another, to ensure the synergy that is necessary for a flourishing mentoring relationship. By taking this approach to encourage professionals to set up their own Personal Boards, organizations can ensure continuity within their organizations from generation to generation and conserve and retain individuals' knowledge and experience within the organization.

STARTING AN OFFICIAL MENTORING PROGRAM

In order to spread the VPBOD system, practitioners should pay it forward not only by serving on Personal Boards but also by spreading the methodology:

- At your organization or workplace.
- As a volunteer at a community or faith-based group.
- At a high school, college, or graduate school.
- Through a professional organization.
- Within your department at work.
- Via social media platforms.

WAYS TO SPREAD THE VPBOD SYSTEM

- Publish articles online, in magazines, in newspapers, or in professional journals.
- Maintain an online blog.
- Discuss the VPBOD system on social media networks.
- Make your Personal Board the subject of lectures or talks.
- Start VPBOD instructional classes at community youth centers.
- Add networking and the VPBOD mentoring model to the curriculum at undergraduate and graduate schools.
- Share your experiences one-on-one with colleagues, friends, family, and other personal associates in a nonprofessional context at social gatherings.
- Suggest to personal friends and family members that they start a VPBOD if they are struggling professionally.
- Pursue a VPBOD-based career-coaching practice, either professionally or as a hobby.

GLOSSARY OF TERMS

ADVANCEMENT CAREER PHASE. The period when you are in passionate pursuit of long-term career objectives. Your position may require that you learn something outside your comfort zone or above your level of expertise, and you have opportunities to proactively learn new skills, take on more responsibilities, and be noticed by higher-ups. During the advancement phase, you may be promoted to a new role in your organization, awarded a more advanced title at a new organization, or make a lateral move to a new service area or field.

BEST SELF. This is achieved when one uses all of one's gifts and talents to manage challenges; the process of functioning at one's greatest potential; someone's journey toward becoming all that he or she can be.

BOOKENDING. The process of informing a supportive person when you begin and end a difficult task. It is an especially useful tool to address procrastination and fear and a powerful way of leveraging your board members. The technique provides structure, a witness to hold you accountable, and support so that you are not alone.

BOSS-MENTOR. A sponsor; boss-mentoring relationships usually end when either the boss or the protégé leaves the organization. Usually, the boss is grooming his or her protégé to succeed him or her, thereby ensuring continuity in the organization.

BOUNDARYLESS CAREER. A term coined by M. B. Arthur and D. M. Rousseau (1996), which involves job opportunities that go beyond single employment settings. It involves the breaking down of traditional boundaries, where careers progress independently of established career paths, boundaries and roles.

CONNECTOR. An individual who has ties in many different realms and acts as a conduit among them, helping to engender connections, relationships, and "cross-fertilization" that otherwise might not have ever occurred.

DEVELOPMENTAL NETWORK. Career developmental assistance from a set, or "constellation," of developmental relationships—from peers, subordinates, friends, family, and bosses; mentoring is received from more than one single person.

eIntroduction. An Internet networking tool, usually a brief message used to introduce two people in your network to each other via the same e-mail, where the connection can be valuable to both parties.

ELEVATOR SPEECH. A short summary used to quickly and simply define a person, profession, product, service, organization, or event and its value proposition; reflects the idea that it should be possible to deliver the summary in the time span of an elevator ride, approximately 30 seconds to two minutes; comes from a scenario of an accidental meeting with someone important in the elevator. If the conversation inside the elevator in those few seconds is interesting and value-adding, the conversation will continue after the elevator ride or end in an exchange of business cards or a scheduled meeting; elevator pitch; elevator statement.

eMentor. The use of technology to expand your mentoring possibilities, by connecting with potential mentors or protégés via social networks, online communities, or other Internet-based communication means.

ESTABLISHMENT CAREER PHASE. When you are looking for or starting your first job or starting out on a new career. At this stage, you need to learn as much as you can about your field, your profession, and the role of your specific title.

GROUP MENTOR. A senior-level executive who mentors a group of junior-level employees; this can take place within the context of an organization or a specific field; especially useful for a mentor who is extremely busy and in high demand by many potential protégés.

INVISIBLE MENTOR. Someone you don't know or cannot access, such as celebrities or hotshots in your field, but whom you can appoint to your personal board.

LATE CAREER PHASE. When a well-established professional is in management or an executive role with authority. The focus is on preserving and perpetuating the work have accomplished over the course of the person's career. Colleagues, coworkers, and subordinates look up to this person as an expert or repository of professional know-how in the field. The person is commended for his or her professional achievements with awards, board positions, and other honors.

MEETING-BEFORE-THE-MEETING. A planning discussion between a mentee and his or her board members in preparation for a difficult meeting.

MENTOR. A resourceful, well-connected supporter; an expert source of coveted information; a wise advisor. A true mentor is, most important, someone who believes in his or her mentee.

MICRO-MESSAGES. Gestures, facial expressions, tones of voice, word choices, eye contact, and interactive nuances that can be either debilitating or empowering to employees and to the power of leadership. Understanding these micro-messages will improve leadership skills.

MIDDLE CAREER PHASE. When a seasoned professional is confident in his or her capabilities, comfortable in the position achieved, and the primary focus is on accomplishment and recognition by peers, colleagues, and higher-ups. Such a person begins mentoring and developing subordinates as a means to pay it forward, prevent career stagnation, and stay in touch with the rank-and-file of the organization.

PEER MENTOR. Fosters peer connections and facilitates dialogue and support among professionals in similar positions and careers.

PROFESSIONAL POSSE. *See* Virtual Personal Board of Directors.

PROTÉGÉ. A mentee.

QUICK CHECK. When a mentee contacts board members quickly for one question that they will be able to answer easily because they know the situation and they know the mentee. Usually, a mentee needs a quick check when there is an urgent task at hand, such as an impending job interview for which he or she needs advice.

REVERSE MENTORING. An initiative in which seasoned executives are paired with and mentored by younger employees on topics such as technology, social media, and current trends.

RULES OF ENGAGEMENT. 17 Rules governing the Virtual Personal Board of Directors methodology.

SPEED MENTORING. A round-robin-style forum in which accomplished female professionals share their experiences with their young counterparts during rapid-fire meetings.

SPONSOR. Someone with influence in a field who can expose a mentee to others who can offer career guidance. Often, sponsor sees that a mentee has promise and feels he or she can open doors to challenging assignments that the mentee might not have been able to get alone. In addition, sponsors will usually protect mentees from negative publicity and may help them to negotiate difficult situations with senior executives and perform other political tasks. Sponsors, more than any other mentor type, are most likely to help someone to get a promotion or initiate an important introduction or connection that leads to a position that would have been completely out of a mentee's reach without the sponsor's assistance.

VIRTUAL PERSONAL BOARD OF DIRECTORS (VPBOD). The functioning body through which an individual may organize a constellation of mentors into a Personal Board.

FURTHER READING

Allen, T. A., Eby, L. T., O'Brien, K. E., & Lentz, E. (2008). The state of mentoring research: A qualitative review of current research methods and future research implications. *Journal of Vocational Behavior, 73,* 343–357.

Ancowitz, N. (2009). *Self-promotion for introverts: The quiet guide to getting ahead.* New York, NY: McGraw-Hill.

Arthur, M. B., & Rousseau, D. M. (1996). *The boundaryless career: A new employment principle for a new organizational era.* New York, NY: Oxford University Press.

Bell, C. R., & Goldsmith, M. (2013). *Managers as mentors: Building partnerships for learning* (3rd ed.). San Francisco, CA: Berrett-Koehler.

Boyer, D., McKenna, P., & Moore, M. (2007). *The power of mentorship and the law of attraction,* special edition.

Bozeman, B., & Feeney M.K. (2007). Toward a useful theory of mentoring: A conceptual analysis and critique. *Administration & Society, 39*(6), 719–739.

Bozionelos, N. (2004). Mentoring provided: Relation to mentor's career success, personality, and mentoring received. *Journal of Vocational Behavior, 64,* 24–46.

Brass, D. J. (1995). A social network perspective on human resources management. *Research in Personnel and Human Resources Management, 13,* 39–79.

Briscoe, J. P., Hall, D. T., & Frautschy DeMuth, R. L. (2006). Protean and boundaryless careers: An empirical exploration. *Journal of Vocational Behavior, 69,* 30–47.

Buckingham, M., & Clifton, D. O. (2001). *Now, discover your strengths.* New York, NY: Free Press.

Burke, R. J., Bristor, J. M., & Rothstein, M. G. (1995). The role of interpersonal networks in women's and men's career development. *International Journal of Career Management, 7*(3): 25–32.

Burke, R. J., McKeen, C. A., & McKenna, C. S. (1993). Correlates of mentoring in organizations: The mentor's perspective. *Psychological Reports, 72,* 883–896.

Burkhardt, M. E. (1994). Social interaction effects following a technological change: A longitudinal investigation. *Academy of Management Journal, 37,* 869–896.

Cain, S. (2012). *Quiet: The power of introverts in a world that can't stop talking.* New York, NY: Crown.

Carlos, D. A. (1990). The impact of race on managers' experiences of developmental relationships (mentoring and sponsorship): An intra-organizational study. *Journal of Organizational Behavior, 11,* 479–492.

Carlos, D. A., & Gabarro, J. J. (1999). *Breaking through: The making of minority executives in corporate America.* Boston, MA: Harvard Business School Press.

Carlos, D. A., & Higgins, M.C. (1996). Mentoring as an extra-organizational activity: Lessons from minority experience. In M. B. Arthur & D. M. Rousseau (Eds.), *The boundaryless career: A new employment principle for a new organizational era.* New York, NY: Oxford University Press.

Carlos D. A., & Kram, K. E. (1988). Promoting career-enhancing relationships in organizations: The role of the human resource professional. In M. London & E. Mone (Eds.), *The human resource professional and employee career development*. New York, NY: Greenwood Press.

Carozza, L. S. (2011). *Science of successful supervision and mentorship*. San Diego, CA: Plural Publishing.

Chao, G. T., Walz, P. M., & Gardner, P. D. (1992). Formal and informal mentorships: A comparison on mentoring functions and contrast with non-mentored counterparts. *Personnel Psychology*, 45(3), 619–637.

Christakis, N. A. (2009). *Connected: The surprising power of our social networks and how they shape our lives—How your friends' friends' friends affect everything you feel, think, and do*. Boston, NY: Little, Brown.

Claman, P. (2010). Employ a personal board of directors. In Harvard Business Review (Ed.), *HBR guide to getting the mentoring you need* (pp. 56–61). New York, NY: Harvard Business Press.

Coutu, D. (2012). What kinds of mentors do you need—and how do you find them? In Harvard Business Review (Ed.), *HBR guide to getting the mentoring you need* (pp. 26–36). New York, NY: Harvard Business Press.

Dreher, G. F., & Ash, R. A. (1990). A comparative study of mentoring among men and women in managerial, professional, and technical positions. *Journal of Applied Psychology*, 75(5), 539–546.

Dries, N., Pepermans, R., & Carlier, O. (2008). Career success: Constructing a multidimensional model. *Journal of Vocational Behavior*, 73, 254–267.

Dutton, J. E., & Ragins, B. R. (2007). *Exploring positive relationships at work: Building a theoretical and research foundation*. Mahwah, NJ: Lawrence Erlbaum Associates.

Eby, L. T. (1997). Alternative forms of mentoring in changing organizational environments: A conceptual extension of the mentoring literature. *Journal of Vocational Behavior*, 51(1), 125–144.

Eby, L. T., & Allen, T. D. (2002). Further investigation of protégés' negative mentoring experiences: Patterns and outcomes. *Group & Organization Management*, 27(4), 456–479.

Eby, L. T., Allen, T. D., Evans, S. C., Ng, T., & DuBois, D. (2008). Does mentoring matter? A multidisciplinary meta-analysis comparing mentored and non-mentored individuals. *Journal of Vocational Behavior*, 72(2), 254–267.

Eby, L. T., Butts, M., Lockwood, A., & Simon, S. A. (2004). Protégés' negative mentoring experiences: Construct development and nomological validation. *Personnel Psychology*, 57(2), 411–447.

Eby, L. T., McManus, S. E., Simon, S. A., & Russell, J. E. A. (2000). The protégé's perspective regarding negative mentoring experiences: The development of a taxonomy. *Journal of Vocational Behavior*, 57(1), 1–21.

Ensher, E., & Murphy, S. (2005). *Power mentoring: How successful mentors and protégés get the most out of their relationships*. San Francisco, CA: Jossey-Bass.

Gallo, A. (2011). Making sure your people succeed: How to set and support employee goals. In Harvard Business Review (Ed.), *HBR guide to giving effective feedback* (pp. 81–89). New York, NY: Harvard Business Press.

Godshalk, V.M., & Sosik, J. J. (2003). Aiming for career success: The role of learning goal orientation in mentoring relationships. *Journal of Vocational Behavior*, 63, 417–437.

Goodyear, M. (2006). Mentoring: A learning collaboration. *Educause Quarterly*, 4, 51–53.

Granovetter, M. S. (1982). The strength of weak ties: A network theory revisited. In P. V. Marsden & N. Lin (Eds.), *Social structure and network analysis* (pp.105–130). Beverly Hills, CA: Sage.

Granovetter, M. S. (1973). The strength of weak ties. *American Journal of Sociology*, 6, 1360–1380.

Hagel, J. III, & Seely Brown, J. (2010). *The Power of pull: How small moves, smartly made, can set big things in action*. New York, NY: Basic Books.

Hansen, M. T., Podolny, J. M., & Pfeffer, J. (2000). *So many ties, so little time: A task contingency perspective on the value of social capital in organizations*. Working paper 00-029. Boston, MA: Harvard Business School.

Harris, C. A. (2009). *Expect to win: 10 proven strategies for thriving in the workplace.* New York, NY: Hudson Street Press.

Hartman, R. L., & Johnson, J. D. (1989). Social contagion and multiplexity: Communication networks as predictors of commitment and role ambiguity. *Human Communication Research, 15,* 523–548.

Harvard Business Review. (2012). Self-assessment: What you don't know about effecting mentoring. In Harvard Business Review (Ed.), *HBR guide to getting the mentoring you need* (pp. 1–4). New York, NY: Harvard Business Press.

Hathaway, R. (2007). *A legacy of faith: A fresh look at blessing, morality, self-worth, and mentorship.* Mustang, OK: Tate Publishing.

Hewlett, S. A., Marshall, M., & Sherbin, L. (2012). The relationship you need to get right. In Harvard Business Review (Ed.), *HBR guide to getting the mentoring you need* (pp. 5–17). New York, NY: Harvard Business Press.

Higgins, M. C. (1999a). *Changing careers: The effects of social context.* Working paper 98016. Boston, MA: Harvard Business School.

Higgins, M. C. (1999b). *When is helping helpful? Effects of evaluation and intervention timing on individual task performance.* Working paper 97-044. Boston, MA: Harvard Business School.

Higgins, M. C. (2000). The more, the merrier? Multiple developmental relationships and work satisfaction. *Journal of Management Development, 19,* 277–296.

Higgins, M. C. (2006). A contingency perspective on developmental networks. In J. Dutton & B. R. Ragins (Eds.), *Exploring positive relationships at work: Building a theoretical and research foundation* (pp. 207–224). Hillsdale, NJ: Lawrence Erlbaum Associates.

Higgins, M. C., Chandler, D., & Kram, K. E. (2007). Boundary spanning of developmental networks: A social network perspective on mentoring. In B. R. Ragins & K. E. Kram (Eds.), *The handbook of mentoring at work: Theory, research, and practice* (pp. 349–372). Thousand Oaks, CA: Sage.

Higgins, M. C., Dobrow, S., & Roloff, K. (2010). Optimism and the boundaryless career: The role of developmental relationships. *Journal of Organizational Behavior, 31*(5), 749–769.

Higgins, M. C., & Kram, K. E. (2001). Reconceptualizing mentoring at work: A developmental network perspective. *Academy of Management Review, 26*(2), 264–288.

Higgins, M. C., & Nohria, N. (1999). The side-kick effect: Mentoring relationships and the development of social capital. In R. Leenders & S. Gabbay (Eds.), *Corporate social capital and liability* (pp. 161–179). Boston, MA: Kluwer Academic Publishers.

Higgins, M. C., & Thomas, D. A. (2001). Constellations and careers: Toward understanding the effects of multiple developmental relationships. *Journal of Organizational Behavior, 22,* 223–247.

Hill, N. (2012). *Napoleon Hill collection.* New York, NY: Penguin.

Hoffman, R., & Casnocha, B. (2012). *The start-up of you.* New York, NY: Crown.

Ibarra, H. (1993). Personal networks of women and minorities in management: A conceptual framework. *Academy of Management Review, 18,* 56–87.

Koberg, C. S., Boss, R. W., Chappell, D., & Ringer, R. C. (1994). Correlates and consequences of protégé mentoring in a large hospital. *Group & Organization Management, 19,* 219–239.

Krackhardt, D., & Porter, L. W. (1985). When friends leave: A structural analysis of the relationship between turnover and stayers' attitudes. *Administrative Science Quarterly, 30,* 242–261.

Krackhardt, D., & Stern, R. N. (1988). Informal networks and organizational crises: An experimental simulation. *Social Psychology Quarterly, 51,* 123–140.

Kram, K. E. (1983). Phases of the mentor relationship. *Academy of Management Journal, 26,* 608–625.

Kram, K. E. (1985). *Mentoring at work: Developmental relationships in organizational life.* Glenview, IL: Scott Foresman.

Kram, K. E. (1986). Mentoring in the workplace. In D. T. Hall (Ed.), *Career development in organizations* (pp. 160–201). San Francisco, CA: Jossey-Bass.

Kram, K. E. (1996). A relational approach to career development. In D. T. Hall (Ed.), *The career is dead— long live the career: A relational approach to careers* (pp. 132–157). San Francisco, CA: Jossey-Bass.

Kram, K. E., & Cherniss, C. (2001). Developing emotional competence through relationships at work. In C. Cherniss & D. Goleman (Eds.), *The emotionally intelligent workplace.* San Francisco, CA: Jossey-Bass.

Kram, K. E., & Hall, D. T. (1996). Mentoring in a context of diversity and turbulence. In E. E. Kossek & S. A. Lobel (Eds.), *Managing diversity: Human resource strategies for transforming the workplace* (pp. 108–136). Cambridge, MA: Blackwell Business.

Kram, K. E., & Isabella, L. A. (1985). Mentoring alternatives: The role of peer relationships in career development. *Academy of Management Journal, 28,* 110–132.

Laird, P. W. (2007). *Pull: Networking and success since Benjamin Franklin (Harvard Studies in Business History).* Boston, MA: Harvard University Press.

Leenders, R. T. A. J., & Gabbay, S. M. (1999). *Corporate social capital and liability.* Boston, MA: Kluwer Academic Publishers.

Lesser, E., & Prusak, L. (2001). Preserving knowledge in an uncertain world. *MIT Sloan Management Review, 43*(1), 101–102.

Lin, N., Ensel, W., & Vaughn, J. C. (1981). Social resources and strength of ties: Structural factors in occupational status attainment. *American Sociological Review, 46,* 393–405.

Locke, E. A. (1976). The nature and causes of job satisfaction. In M. D. Dunnette (Ed.), *Handbook of industrial and organizational psychology.* Chicago, IL: Rand-McNally.

Mannix, E., & Neale, M.A. (2005). What differences make a difference? The promise and reality of diverse teams in organizations. *Psychological Science in the Public Interest, 6*(2), 31–55.

McCauley, C. D., & Young, D. P. (1993). Creating developmental relationships: Roles and strategies. *Human Resource Management Review, 3,* 219–230.

Moon, Y. (2010). *Different: Escaping the competitive herd.* New York, NY: Crown.

Morrison, A. M., & Von Glinow, M. (1990). Women and minorities in management. *American Psychologist, 45,* 200–208.

Mullen, C. A. (2004). *Mentoring Primer (Lang Primers).* New York, NY: Peter Lang International Academic Publishers.

Mullen, C. A., Cox, M. D., Boettcher, C. K., & Adoue, D. S. (1997). *Breaking the Circle of One: Redefining mentorship in the lives and writings of educators. (Counterpoints: Studies in the Postmodern Theory of Education),* 2nd ed. New York, NY: Peter Lang International Academic Publishers.

Noe, R. A. (1988). An investigation of the determinants of successful assigned mentoring relationships. *Personnel Psychology, 41,* 457–479.

Orpen, C. (1995). The effects of mentoring on employees' career success. *Journal of Social Psychology, 135,* 667–668.

Papa, M. J. (1990). Communication network patterns and employee performance with new technology. *Communication Research, 17,* 344–368.

Peters, T. (1999). *The Brand You 50: Or Fifty ways to transform yourself from an 'employee' into a brand that shouts distinction, commitment, and passion!* New York, NY: Knopf.

Pfeffer, J. (1997). *New directions for organization theory: Problems and prospects.* New York, NY: Oxford University Press.

Ragins, B. R. (1997). Antecedents of diversified mentoring relationships. *Journal of Vocational Behavior, 51*(1), 90–109.

Ragins, B. R., & Cotton, J. L. (1993). Gender and willingness to mentor in organizations. *Journal of Management, 19,* 97–111.

Ragins B. R., & Cotton, J. L. (1999). Mentor functions and outcomes: A comparison of men and women in formal and informal mentoring relationships. *Journal of Applied Psychology, 84*, 529–550.

Ragins, B. R., & McFarlin, D. B. (1990). Perceptions of mentor roles in cross-gender mentoring relationships. *Journal of Vocational Behavior, 37*, 321–339.

Raider, H. J., & Burt, R. S. (1996). Boundaryless careers and social capital. In M. B. Arthur & D. M. Rousseau (Eds.), *The boundaryless career: A new employment principle for a new organizational era*. New York, NY: Oxford University Press.

Ralph, E. G., & Walker, K. D. (2011). *Adapting mentorship across the professions: Fresh insights and perspectives*. Edmonton, Alberta: Brush Education.

Rath, T. (2007). *StrengthsFinder 2.0*. New York, NY: Gallup Press.

Reilly, J. M. (1992). *Mentorship: The essential guide for schools and business*. Tucson, AZ: Great Potential.

Roche, G. R. (1979). Much ado about mentors. *Harvard Business Review, 57*(1), 14–28.

Scandura, T. A. (1992). Mentorship and career mobility: An empirical investigation. *Journal of Organizational Behavior, 13*, 169–174.

Singh, R., Ragins, B. R., & Tharenou, P. (2009). What matters most? The relative role of mentoring and career capital in career success. *Journal of Vocational Behavior, 75*, 56–67.

Staley, D., Tracy, B., & Ziglar, G. Z. (2008). *The power of mentorship: Finding your passion.*

Thompson, J. J. (1997). Job prospects are slowly beginning to improve. *U.S. News and World Report, 122*(9), 71–78.

Turban, D. B., & Dougherty, T. W. (1994). Role of protégé personality in receipt of mentoring and career success. *Academy of Management Journal, 37*, 688–702.

Uzzi, B. (1996). The sources and consequences of embeddedness for the economic performance of organizations: The network effect. *American Sociological Review, 61*, 674–698.

Westman, M., & Etzion, D. (1990). The career success/personal failure phenomenon as perceived in others: Comparing vignettes of male and female managers. *Journal of Vocational Behavior, 37*, 209–224.

Wilson, T. D. (2008). *Four stars: Conversations on life, success, leadership, mentorship, culture, and diversity.* Washington DC: Dweylan.

Zachary, L. (2009). *The mentee's guide: Making mentoring work for you.* San Francisco, CA: John Wiley & Sons.

Zerzan, J. T., Hess, R., Schur, E., Phillips, R. S., & Rigotti, N. (2009). Making the most of mentors: A guide for mentees. *Academic Medicine, 84*(1), 140–144.

INDEX